D1135937

PREACHING
AT THE PARISH
COMMUNION

Series 3—Year One (Integrated)

GOSPELS, EPISTLES, COLLECTS

Frank Colquhoun

MOWBRAYS
LONDON & OXFORD

© A. R. Mowbray & Co Ltd 1974

ISBN 0 264 66113 3

First published in 1974
by A. R. Mowbray & Co Ltd
The Alden Press, Osney Mead,
Oxford, OX2 0EG

Text set in 12/13pt. Monotype Bembo, printed by letterpress,
and bound in Great Britain at The Pitman Press, Bath

CONTENTS

iii

*The readings for the five Sundays before Advent Sunday are always to be those provided for Trinity 23 and the four Sundays following. Readings for Trinity 18 to Trinity 22 will be used according as they are needed.

PREFACE

THE SERMON outlines in this book are based on the Sunday readings appended to the Order of Holy Communion Series 3, Table 1. The readings, consisting of Old Testament lesson, Epistle, and Gospel, form a coherent whole and are related to a specific theme for each Sunday. In general I have adhered to the selected theme and where possible I have endeavoured to link the three readings together.

It will be clear that what I am offering here are little more than outlines, not finished sermons. Limitations of space have made it impossible to do anything else. My aim has been to take the biblical material and to expound it in a simple, straightforward way, arranging it under suitable headings. Where they do not appeal, the headings can readily be ignored or altered.

In some instances, as I am well aware, more material is offered than is required for one sermon, especially if it be but a short address at the Parish Communion. But in any case there must be selection and adaptation in the use of these outlines. I would emphasize again that they are not ready-make sermons. The preacher must be prepared to suit them to his own requirements, to reclothe them in living language, to add suitable illustrations, and to apply the message to the particular circumstances and needs of the congregation.

If used in this way I hope the outlines may be of some help to those who, like myself, believe that the day of biblical preaching is not over. Indeed I am convinced that many people in our churches are really more interested in what the Bible has to say on the fundamental issues of life than in our own trivial observations on the passing topics of the day. As preachers we are charged with the ministry of the Word. Let us make full proof of our ministry.

Norwich Cathedral   *Frank Colquhoun*
1974

FOREWORD

AT THE present time, in Church circles, there is an evergrowing interest in the work of the Holy Spirit, the gifts of the Spirit, the effective working of a 'charisma', speaking with tongues and in the Pentecostalist movement generally. It is not surprising therefore, that some preachers today, especially perhaps younger preachers, should give greater prominence to the preparation of the preacher than to the preparation of the sermon, and should wish to give as much room as possible for the freedom of the Spirit in the act of preaching, viewing with some suspicion the work in the study that normally lies behind the preaching of a sermon, all sermons, indeed, that savour of art, or literary style, if not the writing out of a sermon altogether before it is actually delivered in a pulpit.

In this present book of sermon outlines the author grounds his work in Biblical exposition and in Church tradition. I am sure Canon Colquhoun would be second to none in affirming that the ministry of the Word is only effective if it is carried out in and through a reliance on the authority and power of the Holy Spirit. Even if he does not say so explicitly in this book, nevertheless his insistence in his preface that every preacher who uses these sermon outlines must process them for his own use, providing his own illustrations, presupposes this. And we must remember that the Holy Spirit does not only work through a preacher when he stands upon his feet in the pulpit delivering words, but when he sits prayerfully in his study, putting himself in a position to receive and shape for effective communication a word from God for a particular situation.

But there is more to it than this. In I Corinthians 12.28 Paul writes, 'Within our community God has appointed, in the first place apostles, in the second place prophets, thirdly teachers . . .' After the apostles the primacy in the Church is given to prophecy, which means prophecy with interpretation which builds up the life of the Church. All prophecy, all preaching, all teaching, all charismatic action is brought to the bar of this test—does it build up the life of the Church? But note

ix

the juxtaposition of the two that head the list after the apostles, *prophets and teachers*. H. Flender has a striking quotation on this in *Das missionarische Wort* 1/73, 'Prophecy without teaching turns into fanaticism, teaching without prophecy hardens into law'. In this book of sermon outlines the author provides solid Biblical teaching. Time and time again he connects up with a firm historical basis. Let a preacher use this material, let him give place to the dynamic Spirit of God to give it wings, so will sound and effective preaching result, because it will consist of prophecy and teaching which—who can doubt—is in line with the mind of the great apostle St Paul who said, 'It is prophecy that builds up a Christian community'.

Kensington 1974   *D. W. Cleverley Ford*

FIRST SUNDAY IN ADVENT

The Day of the Lord

> 1 Thessalonians 5.2 (NEB) *'You know perfectly well that the Day of the Lord comes like a thief in the night.'*

'You've made my day!' The expression is common enough. It is true, we have our days and some of them mean a great deal to us. God also has *his* day, as the people of the Bible knew well. They spoke about the Day of the Lord. To the Jews in Old Testament times that day meant the time when the Lord would intervene in human affairs and act in righteousness and judgement. Christians in New Testament times also spoke of the Day of the Lord. To them it was the day when the Lord Christ would come again, as he himself had foretold, 'with power and great glory' (see today's Gospel).

In the Epistle St Paul uses the phrase in this sense. By the Day of the Lord he means the second coming of Christ. This was his hope and expectation. As a result a twofold call rings out from this passage.

A call to awake

The Day of the Lord will take men by surprise. It will come 'like a thief in the night'. Jesus said the same (see Luke 12.39). The apostle pictures the world in a state of spiritual darkness, slumbering in sin, dreaming of peace and security (verse 3), unready for the coming of the Lord. 'But you, my friends', he goes on—and now he is addressing believers—'you are not in the dark, that the day should overtake you like a thief. You are all children of light, children of day. We do not belong to night or darkness, and we must not sleep like the rest, but keep awake and sober' (verses 4–6).

The lesson St Paul is pressing home here is that of vigilance. and it's a lesson for ourselves as well as for the Thessalonians. Keep awake! Be on the alert! The call of Advent is a call to watch. How?

(1) We must watch ourselves. We must examine our conduct.

We must cast off the works of darkness. Advent is a penitential season and demands a serious and sober quality of life. Jesus urged his disciples, in the light of his coming, 'Keep a watch on yourselves; do not let your minds be dulled by dissipation and drunkenness and worldly cares so that the great Day closes upon you suddenly like a trap' (St Luke 21.34).

(2) We must watch world events. We must be alert to 'the signs of the times'. We must have our eyes open to what God is doing on the stage of human history. This seems to be the point of the parable of the fig tree in today's Gospel (verses 29–31). Just as the buds are the harbinger of summer, so certain events happening in the world are the precursor of the kingdom of God.

(3) We must watch for the Lord himself. He is the ultimate object of our hope (see Titus 2.13). As Christians we are not merely looking for the coming of the kingdom. We are looking for the coming of the King.

A call to arms

The apostle introduces a new metaphor in his teaching about the Day of the Lord. Before, he has said that Christians must be like a wise householder, watchful, sober and alert. Now he says (verse 8) that those who 'belong to the day' must be like soldiers armed for battle and must 'put on the breastplate of faith and love, and for a helmet the hope of salvation.'

There is no need to attach too much importance to the metaphor of the breastplate and helmet; but perhaps it's worth noting that the first would have protected the soldier's heart and the second his head—the two most vulnerable parts of the body. What is more important is to recognise that Paul views the Christian life not as a cosy armchair religion but as a spiritual conflict, as a battle against the forces of darkness. To watch for the Lord is not enough. We must engage in the holy war. We must heed the call to arms.

The armour is said to represent faith and love and hope. The three are inseparable and interrelated. Faith looks up and lays hold of the unseen Lord. Love looks around and serves those in need. Hope looks forward and anticipates the glory of God. This last point the apostle develops further when he says, 'God has not destined us to the terrors of judgement, but to the full attainment of salvation through our Lord Jesus Christ. He died for us so that we, awake or asleep, might live in company with him' (verses 9, 10).

SECOND SUNDAY IN ADVENT

What about the Old Testament?

> Romans 15.4 (NEB) *'All the ancient scriptures were written for our own instruction.'*

Most Christians appreciate readily enough the value of the New Testament, but they can't always work up much enthusiasm about the Old Testament. 'What's the point of it?' they inquire. 'Isn't it just a record of ancient history or a collection of Jewish folklore? Isn't it quite out of date now as far as we are concerned?'

This is not how the New Testament itself regards the matter, as our text makes clear. The Old Testament was the Bible of the early church, just as it was also our Lord's Bible, and it still has immense value for us. It has a lot to say to us about the purpose of God, the origin of the Church, and the coming of Christ.

The purpose of God

In its opening sentence the Old Testament introduces us to God as the maker of all things: 'In the beginning God created the heavens and the earth.' From that majestic starting point it proceeds to unveil to us the nature of God: his holiness and justice, his wisdom and power, his goodness and grace. It is a gradual and progressive revelation. Little by little the picture becomes clearer as we read on through the historical books and come to the wisdom literature, and finally to the writings of the prophets. At the same time we have unfolded to us God's purpose for the world—for the whole world. For the God revealed in the Old Testament is not a small god, interested in only a section of mankind. He is the God who made the whole

3

earth, who loves all men, and whose design is that people of every race and nation should know him, serve him, and worship him. This tremendous truth rings out in many of the psalms and the writings of the prophets (see today's O.T. lesson, Isaiah 55.4, 5, and the Epistle, vv. 9–12).

How was this worldwide purpose to be realised? Through the Church, God's chosen people Israel.

The people of God

The Church didn't begin on the day of Pentecost, as we sometimes imagine. It was reborn then, with the coming of the Spirit; but it had its birth 2,000 years before with the call of Abraham, and God's promise to him, 'In you all the families of the earth will be blessed'. God chose one nation that through it he might bless all nations.

So the descendants of Abraham were consecrated to be God' people. Later he 'redeemed' or rescued them from Egypt on the fateful passover night. He made a solemn covenant with them. He led them on their journey to the promised land. He gave them his laws. He formed them into a worshipping community, with a divinely appointed priesthood and an elaborate system of sacrifice. This is the beginning of the story of the Jewish church. It is against this background that we can better understand the New Testament teaching about the Christian church.

The tragedy of the Old Testament story is that the Jewish people lost sight of God's worldwide purpose. They became narrow-minded, wrapped up in themselves, and intolerant of those outside the covenant. They failed to fulfil their missionary vocation. They thought that the Lord was exclusively *their* God. They forgot that he was also the God of all men and nations. So God's purpose was temporarily frustrated.

The promise of God

But that purpose was at length fulfilled in the coming of Jesus the Messiah and the creation of the Christian Church, the new Israel. The Messiah's advent had been promised centuries before in the Old Testament. Jesus came according to plan, God's plan, to be the divinely anointed prophet, priest and king, the light of the Gentiles, the one in whom all the families of the earth would be blessed.

This is the golden theme of the ancient scriptures. 'Their testimony points to me,' says Jesus in today's Gospel. 'It was about me that Moses wrote', he claims (John 5.39, 46). In him all the messianic promises find their fulfilment. This is the supreme reason why we as Christians value the Old Testament. It bears witness to our Lord and his saving mission to the world. And we, as members of the new covenant and the new Israel, are necessarily involved with him in that mission.

THIRD SUNDAY IN ADVENT

The testimony of John

> St John 1.19 (RSV) *'This is the testimony of John, when the Jews sent priests and Levites from Jerusalem to ask him, "Who are you?"'*

Last Sunday's Gospel told of our Lord's witness to John the Baptist (John 5.36; see also v.35). Today's Gospel is about John's witness to Jesus. It begins, 'This is the testimony of John'. An official Jewish deputation waited on the Baptist to ask him about himself and his mission. He was extremely reluctant to speak about himself. His immediate answer to his questioners was, 'I am not the Christ'. When pressed further he at last told them who he was—'a voice crying in the wilderness'.

His witness was marked by three things.

John spoke with authority

He spoke with authority because he knew his Bible, the Old Testament scriptures. He had learnt from the Bible the truth about himself. He had learnt it from the passage which forms today's Old Testament lesson. He said, 'I am the voice of one crying in the wilderness, "Make straight the way of the Lord"', as the prophet Isaiah said.' The prophecy is found in Isaiah 40.3.

So John saw that his task was to be the Lord's messenger, to prepare the people for the coming of the Messiah; and with a note of authority he called upon them to repent and to wash away their sins, because the kingdom of heaven was at hand.

John also discovered from the scriptures the truth about Jesus the Messiah. That is why he was able, with the same authority, to bear witness to him as the Lamb of God and the Son of God, the one who bears away the sin of the world and baptises with the Holy Spirit (see vv. 29–34).

John spoke with fidelity

In bearing this witness to Jesus John was utterly faithful. He had no big ideas about himself, but he had very big ideas about Jesus; and it was to Jesus that he was always pointing men. When asked by the Pharisees why he was baptising, if he were not the Messiah, his answer was: 'I baptise in water, but among you, though you do not know him, stands the one who is to come after me' (verses 26, 27). To that unknown figure in their midst John was constantly and faithfully directing his hearers— not to himself. He was nobody. Jesus was everything.

All this reminds us of St Paul's words in today's Epistle: 'This is how one should regard us, as servants of Christ and stewards of the mysteries of God. Moreover it is required of stewards that they be found trustworthy' (1 Corinthians 4.1, 2). John always spoke as Christ's servant. He was a faithful steward.

John spoke with humility

He saw himself to be a very unimportant person. He was merely the baptiser with water. He was not even good enough to unfasten the shoes of Jesus. The only thing he would say about himself was, 'I am a voice crying aloud in the wilderness' (verse 23 NEB).

A voice! That was all John saw himself to be. The function of a voice is to utter words, to convey a message, to speak the truth. This was John's God-given role. He was the herald of the coming Messiah and his voice was lifted up to testify to him and to call upon men to find in him their Saviour and Lord.

6

John spoke with humility. So must we. Our role is to point to the unknown Christ standing in our midst, that men may recognise him, welcome him, and worship him as their King.

> Hark the glad sound! the Saviour comes,
> The Saviour promised long:
> Let every heart prepare a throne,
> And every voice a song.

FOURTH SUNDAY IN ADVENT

The angel's message

> St Luke 1.30–32 (NEB) *'The angel said, "Do not be afraid, Mary, for God has been gracious to you; you shall conceive and bear a son, and you shall give him the name Jesus. He will be great; he will bear the title 'Son of the Most High'; the Lord God will give him the throne of his ancestor David, and he will be king over Israel for ever; his reign shall never end."'*

With Christmas near at hand it is good that we should think today of the amazing message which the angel Gabriel brought to Mary of Nazareth about the child to be born to her and whose birth we are about to celebrate. He addressed her as the 'most favoured one', for the Lord had bestowed on her the highest honour that could befall any woman; yet she was but a lowly, humble village maiden. It is gloriously true, as the Epistle says, that God does not choose the wise, the powerful, and the highly born, but those whom the world regards as 'low and contemptible' to fulfil his designs. So it was in the case of Mary. Listen to what the angel said about her baby.

Mary's child

'You shall conceive and bear a son, and you shall give him the name Jesus.' This is the human side of the picture. The angel's words made three things clear: that the child was to be conceived in Mary's womb; that this child would be a boy; and that he was to be given the name Jesus, meaning saviour or deliverer, the equivalent of the Hebrew name Joshua. These simple facts remind us that there was something very 'ordinary' about the birth of Jesus. He was a truly human child, born of a human mother, and the life he lived in the world was a fully human life.

But that is not the whole picture. The angel had something more to say to Mary.

God's Son

'He will be great; he will bear the title "Son of the Most High".' Jesus was human. He was also divine. The child of Mary was the Son of God. Such is the mystery of the incarnation. It seemed incredible. How could it be?

That was Mary's question. 'How can this be', she asked, 'when I have no husband?' And the answer given by the angel was this: 'The Holy Spirit will come upon you, and the power of the Most High will overshadow you; and for that reason the holy child to be born will be called "Son of God".' The words of Isaiah, foretelling a day when a great light would dawn on the world's darkness, were fulfilled in Jesus:

> 'For to us a child is born,
> To us a son is given.'

What the Church is about to celebrate is not only the birth of a child but the gift of a Son—God's gift, God's Son. When his hour struck, 'God sent his own Son, born of a woman'. The Jesus whom we welcome and worship at Christmas is none other than the eternal Word made flesh.

Israel's Messiah

The angel had something else to say to Mary about her child. 'God will give him the throne of his ancestor David, and he will be king over Israel for ever; his reign shall never end.' Here is a revelation of the royalty of Jesus. It ties up directly with Jewish prophecy. What the angel said in effect was that Mary's baby would be none other than the promised Messiah. Part of that promise is found in today's Old Testament lesson: 'A shoot shall grow from the stock of Jesse, and a branch shall spring from his roots.' Remember, Jesse was the father of David. The Messiah would be of the royal line, great David's greater Son.

This doesn't mean that Jesus came to be merely the Messiah of the Jews; but his mission was 'to the Jew first' and then through the agency of his new Israel, the Church, to the whole world. So we too are involved in God's saving purpose; and as we listen to the angel's message to Mary, focusing our attention as it does on Jesus as our brother Man, the incarnate Son, and the anointed King, we sing for joy at Christmas and like Mary herself we tell out the greatness of the Lord.

SUNDAY AFTER CHRISTMAS

The Man born to be King

> St Matthew 2.1, 2 (NEB) *'Astrologers from the east arrived in Jerusalem, asking, "Where is the child who is born to be king of the Jews?"'*

Jerusalem was in a ferment. Eastern astrologers had arrived in the city announcing the birth of a royal prince of Israel. 'We observed the rising of his star', they declared, 'and we have come to pay him homage.' It was sensational news. Expectations of the coming of the promised Messiah were running high in Jewish circles at the time and doubtless the people of Jerusalem were full of questionings about these men. Who were they? Where had they come from? What did they mean? Had a king of the Jews really been born?

In answering these questions for ourselves let us trace the astrologers' journey, which began in distant eastern lands and ended in Bethlehem, with a halt at Jerusalem en route.

9

Lands of the east

'Astrologers from the east'—that is how the magi or 'wise men' are described in the NEB. From what eastern land they had come we are not told. Quite likely it was Arabia or Persia, but in any case it is not important. What is important is that they were Gentiles, not Jews. This is the chief significance of their appearance in this strongly Jewish gospel of Matthew. It is as though the evangelist wishes to remind his readers at the outset of his story that Jesus is not only the Jewish Messiah but also the Saviour of the world. So the magi represent the Gentiles (or nations) seeking Christ and being drawn into the light of his salvation.

Here is the beginning of the fulfilment of the ancient prophecy which forms today's Old Testament lesson: 'Arise, shine, for your light has come, and the glory of the Lord has risen upon you . . . And nations shall come to your light, and kings to the brightness of your rising' (Isaiah 60.1, 3). It is probably this prophecy that gave rise to the dubious tradition that the magi were kings.

City of Jerusalem

From eastern lands we move on to the city of Jerusalem. It is hardly surprising that Herod was 'greatly perturbed' when he learned of the arrival of the astrologers with their question, 'Where is the child who is born to be king of the Jews?' After all, Herod considered that *he* was the king of the Jews. Was this child a rival to his throne? If so, he must be eliminated as speedily as possible. Herod was that sort of man, as history testifies— ruthless, crafty, and insanely jealous. His first step was to ask the Jewish religious experts, 'Where is it that the Messiah is to be born?' In answering his question it is noteworthy that the priests and scribes did not consult the heavenly bodies, as the magi had done. They had a brighter light to guide them. They turned not to the stars but to the scriptures, referring Herod to Micah's prophecy that it was from Bethlehem in Judah that Israel's ruler should come (Micah 5.2).

One special lesson emerges from this part of the story. The Bible is the book that answers our questions. In particular it answers our questions about Jesus Christ and consistently points us to him as our Saviour and King.

Little town of Bethlehem

At Herod's behest the eastern pilgrims made their way to Bethlehem where eventually their long quest ended. The star they had seen at its rising reappeared and guided them to the right house; and entering it they found the newborn King, bowed in homage before him, and offered him their gifts: gold, frankincense, and myrrh. Perhaps we are justified in regarding these offerings as 'solemn gifts of mystic meaning', for the story as a whole contains various symbolical elements. But we are on more solid ground if we say that the gifts of the magi were the choicest products of the distant lands from which they came, and that as such they were gifts worthy of a king.

Today, Jesus claims *our* homage and worship and is worthy of the best we can give him. For as the Epistle makes clear, he is at once our Prophet, through whom God has spoken his final word to men; our Priest, who has offered the perfect sacrifice to purge our sins; and our King, who has taken his seat at the right hand of the Majesty on high. So we too worship the Lord in the beauty of holiness.

SECOND SUNDAY AFTER CHRISTMAS

The law and the gospel

St Luke 2.30 (RSV) '*Mine eyes have seen thy salvation.*'

Nearly all religions have their particular ceremonies associated with the birth of a child. It is so in our Christian religion. It is also so in the religion of the Jews. That is why when Jesus was born, as St Luke carefully explains at the beginning of today's Gospel, certain things were done to him in accordance with the

Mosaic law. At the same time, as we read later in the passage, certain things were said about him with reference to the destiny he was to fulfil. So in considering these matters we are pointed back to the past and directed forward to the future.

The old order fulfilled

First we look back and consider the ceremonies described in verses 21–24. Three are mentioned. *First,* there was the circumcision of the child on the eighth day. By this means he was brought within the Jewish covenant. He was also given his human name Jesus; and Luke reminds us that this was 'the name given by the angel before he was conceived'. *Second,* there was the redemption of the firstborn, in recognition of the fact that every firstborn son was regarded as 'holy', that is, belonging to the Lord. The parents were required, so to speak, to purchase their child back by paying the shekel of the sanctuary, and then to 'present him to the Lord', rather as Hannah had done in the case of Samuel. (See Old Testament lesson; also Exodus 13.1, 2, 13; Numbers 18.16) *Third,* there was the purification of the mother after childbirth. This was accomplished by two burnt offerings: 'a pair of turtle doves or two young pigeons' (for details, see Leviticus 12).

These ceremonies were all part of the ancient Mosaic law, as the evangelist states. They may not have much meaning for us today; but the point is that Jesus was born into the Jewish order and under the Jewish law, with a view to establishing a bigger and better order for mankind.

The new order foretold

So now we turn from the things done to the infant Jesus to the things said about him. And here we leave behind the observance of the law and listen to the voice of prophecy. The spokesman is Simeon, that devout and upright old man, who had been promised that he would not see death till he had seen the Messiah. That day, led by the Spirit to the temple, he took Mary's child into his arms and knew that God's promise to him had been fulfilled:

'For mine eyes have seen they salvation
which thou hast prepared in the presence of all
    peoples,
a light for revelation to the Gentiles,
and the glory of thy people Israel.'

The great truth Simeon disclosed in his *Nunc Dimittis* was
that Jesus was to inaugurate a new order and a new covenant,
embracing all nations, Gentiles as well as Jews. In his later words
to Mary (verses 34, 35) he also foreshadowed the cross and the
bitter pain that she herself would share: 'This child is destined
to be a sign which men reject; and you too shall be pierced to the
heart.' That prophecy was fulfilled on Good Friday; and it was
through the agonising events of Good Friday that God's saving
purpose for all mankind was accomplished.

'Mine eyes have seen thy salvation.' Simeon could say that
because he had looked into the face of the baby lying in his arms.
We too by faith can embrace the Lord Jesus. We too by faith
can see in him the salvation of God.

FIRST SUNDAY AFTER EPIPHANY

The baptism of Jesus

St Matthew 3.13 (NEB) *'Jesus arrived at the Jordan from
Galilee, and came to John to be baptised by him.'*

Why did Jesus ask for baptism? Perhaps it sounds a simple
enough question, but it's worth remembering that even John
himself found it something of a problem. He was most reluctant
to baptise Jesus. To him the idea seemed quite incongruous.
'Do you come to me?' he said to Jesus; 'I need rather to be
baptised by you.' As we think about the matter for ourselves
let us see what meaning we can discover in the familiar story.
Here are four key words which may help.

Identification

In his baptism Jesus made himself one with sinful men. John was right in raising his objection. His baptism with water signified the washing away of sin. It was for those who were prepared to confess their sins, turn from them, and receive God's forgiveness. But Jesus was without sin. In this he differed from the rest of mankind. Why then should he be baptised? In submitting to the ordinance he was taking his stand by the side of the sinners he had come to save. His baptism revealed his love for them. It was an act of self-identification. At Jordan, as later at Calvary, he was 'numbered with the transgressors'.

Dedication

His baptism marked the beginning of our Lord's public ministry. At that solemn moment he was offering his life to God for the work he had come to fulfil. That work was none other than the redemption of the world: the work that would make possible in human experience what John's baptism could only signify, the washing away of sin. This is man's fundamental need, the gospel's primary offer. In today's Epistle we listen to the apostle Peter preaching that gospel in the house of Cornelius, pointing to Jesus' death and resurrection and declaring, 'Everyone who trusts in him receives forgiveness of sins through his name.' To make that possible was the supreme purpose of our Lord's ministry on earth; and his baptism was in a sense his ordination to this ministry. So it was not only an act of self-identification. It was also an act of self-dedication.

Investiture

Jesus was the Messiah. The word Messiah means *anointed*. At his baptism he was anointed for his messianic mission. At the moment he came up out of the water heaven opened and 'he saw the Spirit of God descending like a dove to alight upon him'. For Jesus the vision was a flash of divine revelation in response to the dedication of his life to the Father's will and purpose. Like kings of old, he was anointed for service (see Old Testament lesson). And so, as it has been said, 'The endowment of the Spirit is to be interpreted as the investiture of Jesus, with a view to the fulfilment of his messianic mission, with the plentitude of of supernatural authority and power' (A. E. J. Rawlinson).

Attestation

The final act of the baptismal drama was the voice from heaven. The years of obscurity Jesus had passed at Nazareth—the silent years as they have been called—were over. At his baptism the silence was broken and his identity disclosed. 'A voice from heaven was heard saying, "This is my Son, my Beloved, on whom my favour rests."' So in beginning his ministry among men Jesus was not only anointed with the Spirit but also attested of the Father. His baptism gave him a fresh assurance of his divine sonship. It was with that assurance that he went forth from his baptism to finish the work the Father had given him to do.

SECOND SUNDAY AFTER EPIPHANY

Follow me

> St Mark 1.16, 17 (RSV) *'Passing along by the Sea of Galilee Jesus saw Simon and Andrew his brother casting a net in the sea, for they were fishermen. And he said to them, "Follow me, and I will make you become fishers of men."'*

Last Sunday's Gospel was about the baptism of Jesus when he dedicated his life to his public ministry. In today's Gospel we see him entering upon his work, preaching the good news of God's kingdom and urging men to repent and believe. But Jesus cannot accomplish the whole work himself. He needs companions, partners in service, men who will carry on the work in the future. So here we have the record of the call of the first disciples. Let us take a look at them.

The men Jesus chose

What sort of men did Jesus choose? The first were two pairs of brothers, Peter and Andrew, and James and John, who were fishermen on the Sea of Galilee. There's quite a lot we might say about them. For one thing, they were almost certainly young men, like Jesus himself—a point not to be overlooked. More important, the fact that they were fishermen means that they were not upper class but ordinary working men, tough and strong and ready to face a hard life. This too is worth noting in a day when the Church has so largely lost touch with the masses and become bourgeois. Christianity began as a working-class movement. Again, these men Jesus chose and who later became his apostles were Galileans: people with a wider and more cosmopolitan outlook than the Judeans. Men from 'Galilee of the Gentiles' were just the type to form the nucleus of a world-wide church whose mission was to embrace all nations.

The challenge he gave them

'Follow me and I will make you become fishers of men.' Such was the call Jesus addressed to these fishermen. It was clear and uncompromising; what did it imply? For instance, what does it mean to *follow*? Perhaps the NEB helps us here: 'Come with me'. When Jesus called men to follow him he was challenging them not only to imitate him but to join his company and to share his life. 'Follow *me*'—it was a very personal call. Jesus invited people to attach themselves to him, not to a cause or a movement. This is the essence of Christian faith. Discipleship means a personal encounter with Jesus Christ. The story of the conversion of Saul of Tarsus (today's Epistle) illustrates the point. And discipleship involves evangelism: 'I will make you to become fishers of men.' That also was true in the case of Saul, who became Paul the apostle.

The response he received

It was a decisive moment for these Galilean fishermen. They could not evade the issue. They had to say Yes or No to Jesus and act accordingly. Their response was wholehearted. Peter and Andrew 'at once left their nets and followed him'. James and John did the same: 'leaving their father Zebedee in the boat with the hired men, they went off to follow him'. It was a costly decision. It involved considerable sacrifice: giving up their jobs, forsaking home and family, and facing a hazardous future. But these men had already got to know Jesus (see John 1) and they were convinced they could trust him. So in faith they committed themselves to his service. Let us do the same.

> In simple trust like theirs who heard,
>   Beside the Syrian sea,
> The gracious calling of the Lord,
> Let us, like them, without a word
>   Rise up and follow thee.

THIRD SUNDAY AFTER EPIPHANY

The difference Christ makes

St John 2.13 '*This deed at Cana-in-Galilee is the first of the signs by which Jesus revealed his glory and led his disciples to believe in him.*'

St John consistently describes our Lord's miracles as 'signs' because they *signify* something. They are not only works of supernatural power; they are also parables in action, fraught with deep spiritual meaning. What significance are we to attach to this first sign, the turning of the water into wine at Cana? Archbishop William Temple suggested that the incident illustrates 'the difference that Christ makes'. The story is certainly worth thinking about from this point of view. The Lord Jesus does make an enormous difference whenever and wherever he comes, as this narrative more than hints.

By his coming into our world

We begin by noting the difference Christ makes by his coming into our world in visible human form (see today's Epistle). Why was the Life manifested? One answer is this: Jesus came to abolish the old order of the law and to establish a new order of grace. In a word, he came to change the very basis of religion as it then existed. That change is exemplified by the transforming of the water into wine at the wedding feast. It is not far-fetched to see in the water a symbol of Judaism, for as the evangelist explains, the water was 'the kind used for Jewish rites of purification'. And still more obviously is the wine of a sign of the redemption which the Lord Jesus wrought for us by his cross; for at the last supper he took the wine cup and gave it to the disciples with the words, 'This is my blood, the blood of the covenant, shed for many for the forgiveness of sins.'

As a result of the coming of Jesus—his life and death and resurrection—the old covenant is superseded by the new. The law gives place to the gospel, and man's relationship with God is now founded on grace, not on works. This is one difference that Christ makes and it is one element in the glory which he revealed at Cana.

By his coming into our homes

Again, what a difference Christ makes when he comes into our homes! The story has something to say about that; for the background is a village wedding and the scene is set in a home. In the midst of the festivities a domestic crisis occurs: 'the wine gave out'. It was a most embarrassing moment. What was to be done? We do not know what would have happened in other circumstances, but in this instance the crisis was resolved because Jesus was there as one of the invited guests. Mary his mother does the most sensible thing: she tells him about the problem. She does not dictate to him what action he should take. She is content to leave the matter entirely in his hands, knowing that he will do what is best. That is why she says to the servants, 'Do whatever he tells you.'

Domestic problems are not unknown to those of us who are Christians; but it makes all the difference in the life of the home when we have the Lord with us and can talk to him about our troubles. 'Tell Jesus' is the best possible advice when there is trouble at home. In 1845 a young Irishman Joseph Scriven left his native land to settle in Canada. News reached him there that his widowed mother was passing through a time of special sorrow. To comfort her he wrote some verses and sent them to her. They are the lines beginning 'What a Friend we have in Jesus'. They have brought comfort to many hearts and homes since then:

> Have we trials and temptations?
> Is there trouble anywhere?
> We should never be discouraged:
> Take it to the Lord in prayer.

By his coming into our lives

This is the personal aspect of the matter. When Jesus revealed his glory at Cana something happened in the lives of his disciples: they were led to *believe in him*. Of course they had believed before in a sense, for they were already 'disciples' (learners); but now their faith went deeper. The phrase used indicates that at this point they committed themselves to Jesus in complete trust. The revelation of his glory resulted in a new experience of his grace. So the story of the changing of the water into wine shows the difference Christ makes in our lives when we really trust him. He not only changes things: he changes people. He enriches life; he brings fullness of joy. The story, looked at from this angle, portrays the transforming power of Christ who came that we might have life, and life abundant.

FOURTH SUNDAY AFTER EPIPHANY

Friend of sinners

> St Mark 2.17 (NEB) '"*It is not the healthy that need a doctor, but the sick; I did not come to invite virtuous people, but sinners.*"'

One of the accusations often flung at Christians today was never directed towards our Lord: the accusation of snobbishness. In fact he was charged with the opposite fault. The Pharisees criticised him for keeping bad company, mixing too freely with 'tax-gatherers and sinners'—that is, the social outcasts. We have an instance of that in today's Gospel, arising from the call of Levi the tax collector. The story consists of two parts. In the first part Jesus *gives* an invitation and Levi follows him: in the second he *accepts* an invitation and dines at Levi's house.

The invitation Jesus gave

The Lord had been speaking to great crowds by the lakeside at Capernaum. When he had finished he passed by the custom-house where this man Levi was at work. His business was to collect taxes (for the Romans) levied on goods passing through Capernaum on the highway that ran from Damascus to the coast. It was a sordid sort of job for a Jew to get mixed up with, for the whole system was based on exploitation and fraud and meant making money by fleecing one's fellow countrymen. Small wonder the tax-gatherers were thoroughly detested and scorned and ostracised by loyal Jews. Yet here was Jesus actually inviting one of these men to join him in his work. 'Follow me!' was his peremptory call to Levi. We must not make the mistake of thinking that this was Levi's first encounter with Jesus. Obviously enough he had already come into touch with the young Galilean prophet and had felt the impact of his personality and teaching. Now came the decisive moment, the definite invitation. Levi must have been astonished. Other religious teachers would have nothing to do with him. But Jesus wanted him—and wanted him there and then. Levi did not hesitate: he rose and followed him.

Why did Jesus choose and call Levi? For two reasons at least, we may suppose. First and formeost because he loved him, with that free and bountiful love that God has for all sinners (see O.T. lesson); and second, because he needed him—just as also, of course, Levi needed Jesus. The Lord's invitation to him was a call to service; for Levi, whom we know better by his new name, Matthew ('gift of God'), had a great job to do for Jesus and became a powerful agent in the propagation of the gospel.

The invitation Jesus accepted

We know Levi or Matthew as an evangelist. His name confronts us on the first page of the New Testament. He made it his business to share the good news about Jesus, and it seems that he did this from the very beginning. His first piece of evangelism took place immediately after his call. He 'held a big reception in his house for Jesus', so St Luke tells us, and 'among the guests was a large party of tax-gatherers and others'—Levi's old colleagues and companions. It was his way of introducing them to his new master.

The Pharisees were immediately up in arms. In their eyes it was a scandalous thing for Jesus to defy convention and accept Levi's invitation to a reception composed of rogues and renegades. 'Why do you eat and drink with tax-gatherers and sinners?' they asked. The answer Jesus gave is significant, for in it he not only justified his conduct but also defined his mission. The people with whom he was mingling *were* 'sinners'—yes, he admitted it. But these were the very people he had come to seek and to save. 'It's not the healthy who need a doctor', he declared, 'but the sick. My mission is to the sick in soul, not to those who think they are all right.' In saying that he rebuked the self-righteous Pharisees who had no sense of their spiritual ills. At the same time he held out hope and encouragement to the guests in Levi's house. Desperately sick they might be, but they had not been abandoned. The Great Physician had come to them in their need to assure them of God's grace, to call them to repentance, and to offer them life and health and peace. Such was the good news of the kingdom then. Such is still the good news today.

FIFTH SUNDAY AFTER EPIPHANY

The Bridegroom

St Mark 2.19 (NEB) *'Jesus said to them, "Can you expect the bridegroom's friends to fast while the bridegroom is with them? As long as they have the bridegroom with them, there can be no fasting."'*

Jesus had more trouble with the Pharisees, the ultra-religious people of his day, than with any other section of the community. They were constantly finding fault with him, questioning his teaching, passing judgement on his actions. This chapter of Mark's Gospel contains several examples of that sort. Here their criticism arises out of the question of fasting (see verse 18). How does the Lord reply to their complaint?

The newness of the gospel

In dealing with the matter of fasting Jesus makes perfectly plain that the fundamental issue here is the contrast between the religion of law (represented by the Pharisees) and the good news of the kingdom of grace which he was proclaiming. This is the point of the two little parables at the end of the passage about the old coat and the old wineskin. The 'old' in each case symbolises the Jewish faith; the 'new' pictures the gospel. Christianity is not a patched-up Judaism: it is a new garment, the garment of salvation (Isaiah 61.10). The old forms and ceremonies of the Mosaic economy cannot contain the fresh, fermenting wine of the Spirit. 'Jesus was introducing something so absolutely new and revolutionary that he could not be expected to try to accommodate it to the standard religious practices of the Jews' (C. F. D. Moule). As another commentator says, 'You cannot

22

combine Law and Grace' (A. M. Hunter). The gospel is new news as well as good news.

The joy of the kingdom

When Jesus wishes to describe the character of the kingdom of God he speaks of it in terms of a wedding feast. Hence his immediate answer to the question of the Pharisees: 'Can you expect the bridegroom's friends to fast while the bridegroom is with them?' By the bridegroom Jesus means, of course, himself, and the bridegroom's friends are the company of his disciples. It is a marvellous description. The whole picture set before us is that of a wedding party with all the hilarity and merriment associated with such an occasion. So the true symbol of the kingdom is not fasting but feasting. Its pervasive spirit is not gloom but gladness. What Jesus is saying in pictorial language is that the Messianic Age has come and that the banquet of the kingdom has been spread and a good time is being had by all. For the kingdom of God is joy in the Holy Spirit (Romans 14.17).

The presence of the bridegroom

This joy of the kingdom is due to one factor, and one factor alone: the presence of the bridegroom. 'As long as they have the bridegroom with them', says Jesus, 'there can be no fasting.' This is the secret. And Jesus himself, as we have seen, is the bridegroom. It is his presence that makes all the difference. But what are we to make of the saying here, 'The time will come when the bridegroom will be taken away from them, and on that day they will fast'? The reference is not, as we might suppose, to the time when Jesus would leave this world and return to the Father. No. He is speaking rather of the cross. He already foresees the day when for a while he will be 'snatched away' from his friends and they will be plunged into grief. And so it was, as we know. But with the resurrection they were reunited with their living Lord and given the assurance, 'I am with you always, to the end of time.' As Christians we are living in the age of the

Spirit, the age not of the Bridegroom's absence but of his presence; and in his presence there is fullness of joy.

SIXTH SUNDAY AFTER EPIPHANY

Mr Legality

> St Mark 1.27 (RSV) *'Jesus said to them, "The sabbath was made for man, not man for the sabbath."'*

In the early pages of Bunyan's *Pilgrim's Progress* we meet with a certain gentleman called Mr Legality, who dwelt under the shadow of Mount Sinai. Christian was directed to his house by Worldly Wiseman, who described Legality as 'a very judicious man' and one that had 'skill to help men off with their burdens'. Alas, poor Christian found no relief from his own burden in that quarter. The terrors of the law overwhelmed him and he was taught the painful lesson that the law is powerless to justify the sinner.

In the gospel records Mr Legality often appears in the person of the Pharisees, who are prominent figures in today's Gospel. As we read these stories it is not difficult to see why Jesus found fault with their legalistic outlook.

A false emphasis on externals

For one thing, they placed a false emphasis on the mere externals of religion. In fact their religion tended to be all on the outside, something to be seen by men, rather than the hidden religion of the heart. On the question of sabbath observance, as the stories before us make clear, the Pharisees were concerned only with trivialities. They condemned the disciples of Jesus for plucking ears of corn and asserted that they were doing something that was forbidden on the sabbath, namely, reaping. They failed to see that the sabbath law had an inner meaning and went much deeper than mere outward actions. Today's Old Testament lesson reminds us that the same sort of thing was true in Isaiah's day: the formalities of religion were gone through but the spiritual dimension was lacking (Isaiah 1.10–17).

A wrong view of the law

In finding fault with the disciples for plucking and eating ears of corn the Pharisees showed they had a mistaken view of the law. This was another point Jesus made. *Why* did the disciples pluck the corn? Not to amuse themselves but because they were feeling hungry (see St Matthew 12.1). In other words they were doing what they did on the sabbath in order to satisfy a legitimate human need; and Jesus justified their action on that ground. He pointed the Pharisees to the example of the great King David: when he and his men were hungry they had actually eaten the 'holy bread' of the sanctuary which, by the law, was reserved for the priests alone. So now he declared, 'The sabbath was made for man, not man for the sabbath.' He was making clear the law's true design. It was framed not for its own sake but for the benefit of man, for his total well-being in body, mind and spirit. This was specially true of the sabbath law. It was meant to be a blessing, not a burden; and human need always has priority over legal maxims.

A sad lack of compassion

Legalism, with its stress on the letter of the law, makes for hardness. The story of the man with the withered arm illustrates this. The critics of Jesus had no concern for the man. They displayed a quite heartless attitude towards him. They didn't really care whether he was healed or not. All that concerned them was to frame a charge against Jesus. When challenged by him about doing good on the sabbath they had nothing to say (verse 4). That is why, before curing the man, Jesus 'looked around at them with anger, grieved at their hardness of heart'. These men had come to the synagogue that sabbath not to worship but simply to criticise. The sight of the sufferer awakened no compassion. Their interest was in legality, not in humanity. No wonder Jesus was angry. *He* believed in the value of *people*. To him people mattered more than sabbatarian rules and regulations. Clearly Mr Legality has no part in the kingdom of grace.

SEPTUAGESIMA SUNDAY

The Master

> St Matthew 5.1, 2 (RSV) *'Seeing the crowds, Jesus went up on the mountain, and when he sat down his disciples came to him. And he opened his mouth and taught them.'*

Christians often speak of Jesus as 'the Master', especially Christians of the older generation. The title is largely derived from the Authorised Version where it is frequently used as a translation of the word *didaskolos*, meaning properly 'teacher'. The corresponding word for his followers is *mathetes*, 'disciples' or scholars. Clearly the language is that of the class room. It reminds us that we are learners in the school of Christ and that he is our Master, our Teacher, who reveals to us God's truth.

Today's Gospel presents him to us in this capacity. It also provides a familiar example of his teaching.

Looking at the Master

The passage begins with a vivid word picture. We see Jesus going up the 'mountain' or hill in Galilee to teach his disciples as they gather round him. Note the description 'when he sat down': the usual posture adopted by the Jewish rabbi when teaching. Many commentators consider that the evangelist is drawing a parallel between the action of Jesus here and that of Moses when he promulgated the ancient law from Mount Sinai: that he is deliberately portraying Jesus as the second and greater Moses. This may well be so; but we must remember that the new righteousness of the kingdom which Jesus proclaims is basically different from the law of the old covenant. 'The precepts of Christ are not statutory definitions like those of the Mosaic code, but indications of *quality* and *direction* of action which may be present at quite lowly levels of performance' (C. H. Dodd).

Listening to the Master

So the scene is set, and our eyes see our Teacher, as the Old Testament lesson says. Now we listen to what he has to say. The opening part of this discourse which we know as the Sermon on the Mount consists of the beatitudes. It is significant that whereas the sermon as a whole has to do with conduct—the ethics of the kingdom—the beatitudes are concerned primarily with *character*. Conduct is determined by character; so Jesus begins by describing the kind of people who receive the blessing of the Lord. The 'blessed' are those who are blessed by God. The term means much more than mere happiness.

To whom is God's blessing given? First, to the 'poor in spirit': to those who acknowledge their spiritual poverty and cast themselves upon his grace. Those who 'mourn' are the penitents who sorrow for sin, their own and that of the world. The 'meek' are the truly humble in heart who submit to the will of God. Those who 'hunger and thirst for righteousness' are the people who long and labour to see right prevail and evil overthrown. The 'merciful' are those of a generous and forgiving spirit. The 'pure in heart' are people who are clean *inside*. The 'peacemakers' are those who exercise a ministry of reconciliation in human life. It is a wonderful character that is here presented; but people of this kind are not likely to be popular in a world with quite opposite standards and ideals, and so the two final beatitudes refer to the blessing promised to those who endure persecution for the sake of Christ and the kingdom.

Learning from the Master

As we thus listen to the Master the question we must ask is What does this mean for ourselves today? In what ways do these beatitudes speak to our condition? It is not enough simply to listen to the Master. We must be ready to learn from him and apply what he teaches us to our own lives. For example, how far do we really hunger and thirst to see right prevail? And what about the quality of mercy? Have we learned to forgive those who trespass against us? Or again, are we true peacemakers and reconcilers, or do we tend to create discord and division? These are searching questions. One thing is clear. If we listen with honest hearts to our Teacher we shall find that he is saying to us again and again, 'This is the way, walk in it' (Isaiah 30.21).

SEXAGESIMA SUNDAY

The Great Physician

> St Mark 2.5 (NEB) 'When Jesus saw their faith, he said to the paralysed man, "My son, your sins are forgiven."'

Last Sunday's Gospel gave us a picture of Jesus as teacher. Today's Gospel shows him in the capacity of healer. It is good that we should view these two aspects of his ministry together, for his work of healing illustrates his message. The great theme of his teaching was the kingdom of God: the healing miracles are 'signs' of the kingdom. Not only do they arise out of his compassion for suffering humanity. They are also in harmony with his purpose to further the will of God in a sin-sick world. And God's will is certainly health, not disease; life, not death. The story of the paralytic is in many ways typical of our Lord's mission as the Great Physician.

Making men whole

In his healing ministry Jesus was concerned with the whole of man's personality: body, mind and spirit. He didn't make an artificial distinction between one and the other or divide human life into separate compartments. It has been wisely said: 'The healing miracles were no mere incidental works of pity, but the fruit of Jesus' strong conviction that he had come into the world to redeem our human personality in all its aspects, physical as well as spiritual, and to offer to God his Father whole men' (James Stewart). The story before us exemplifies this. The man brought to Jesus was suffering from paralysis, a physical disability; yet the first word the Lord spoke to him was about the patient's spiritual condition: 'My son, your sins are forgiven.' He saw that bodily healing without spiritual health is not sufficient and does not represent God's redeeming purpose for our lives.

The factor of faith

'When Jesus saw their faith'—that is, the faith of the four men who had brought their friend to him. How did he see their faith? By what they did. The trouble they took and the obstacles they overcame to get the paralysed man into the presence of Jesus proved their faith; for faith without works is dead. This factor of faith is present in nearly all the acts of healing related in the gospels. 'According to your faith let it be done' are characteristic words of Jesus. 'Your faith has saved you', he said to more than one sufferer. 'Fear not, only have faith', he assures Jairus. The point is that the miracles of healing are not pieces of magic, wrought irrespective of the moral and spiritual condition of those in need. Faith represents the element of human response and co-operation. It opens a door by which God's power can enter our lives. On the other hand unbelief raises a barrier to that power.

Divine authority

The Lord's words of absolution to the paralytic were challenged by the scribes. 'Why does this fellow talk like that?' they asked. 'This is blasphemy! Who but God alone can forgive sins?' The question embodied an undeniable truth. Jesus answered it in a visible deed, not simply in an audible word. He demonstrated his authority to forgive sins (the spiritual side) by his power to heal the sick (the physical side); and he did this in his capacity as the 'Son of Man'. The latter is a messianic title, derived from the Old Testament. Jesus was more than man. He was the Lord's Anointed, and in him the power of God was uniquely present, unimpeded by human sin and disobedience.

Here is the key to the healing ministry of Jesus and to all his mighty works. The key is the Incarnation, as a result of which he both spoke and acted with divine authority.

QUINQUAGESIMA SUNDAY

The five thousand

> St John 6.5 (NEB) *'Jesus said to Philip, "Where are we to buy bread to feed these people?"'*

What are we to make of the miracles of Jesus? The healing miracles are probably not so much of a problem, but the so-called nature miracles (such as the feeding of the five thousand) are a stumbling-block to many. Two things may by said of the miracles in general. First, they are an important and integral element in the gospel records, and part of the earliest tradition; which means that they cannot be ignored, or eliminated, or explained away. Second, the greatest miracle in the gospels is Jesus Christ himself, the uniqueness of his person as the Word made flesh. He is greater than all his works; and his perfect and sinless life is as big a miracle in the moral sphere as any of his mighty acts in the physical realm.

Against this background let us look at the story of the five thousand. There are two sides to it, the human and the divine. We will take each in turn.

The human side: scarcity

The human side is marked by scarcity. At the outset we are confronted by a mass of human need. Here are thousands of hungry people who, as the other gospels make clear, had spent the day listening to the teaching of Jesus. Now evening is drawing on. What is to be done for them? Jesus challenges Philip on the subject: Where are we to buy bread to feed these people?' The object of the question was to test Philip's faith. Alas, his faith did not rise very high. His answer (verse 7) shows that he was looking at the situation simply from the financial point of view. To him, it was all a matter of money. He said in effect, 'Lord, if only we had the cash all would be well!' There are a good many people today who think that money is the answer to every problem.

Then Andrew appeared on the scene. Evidently he had been

carrying out some inquiries among the crowd to find out what food was available, and now he reported to Jesus, 'There is a boy here who has five barley loaves and two fishes; but what is that among so many?' His words reveal the total inadequacy of the human resources. Five loaves to feed five thousand! The idea was ludicrous in the extreme.

The only bright spot in the story from the human angle is the 'little lad' whom Andrew introduced to Jesus. It seems that he was willing to part with his picnic lunch and hand it over to Jesus. It was an amazingly generous and unselfish act on the boy's part. No doubt it was inspired by Jesus himself. The boy had been gripped by the Lord's teaching and knew that here was someone he could trust. He had little to offer, but he gave what he had (cf. today's Epistle: the Philippians' gift to St Paul in prison).

The divine side: sufficiency

Jesus accepted and used the gift offered to him. So we turn to the other side of the story; and now there is sufficiency. Jesus at once took charge and showed himself master of the situation. That is demonstrated in the charge he gave to the disciples, 'Make the people sit down.' Then with the food put at his disposal the Lord proceeded to feed the vast throng. The picture is full of instruction. For one thing, it shows us divine love in action; for behind the work performed was the Lord's deep concern and compassion for the hungry multitude.

But more: what his love willed his creative power made possible. That a supernatural work was performed is beyond question. To try to rationalise the incident and suggest that the people were simply persuaded to imitate Jesus' example and share their food with one another is both puerile and dishonest. As William Temple commented: 'It is clear that every Evangelist supposed our Lord to have worked a creative act; and for myself I have no doubt that this is what occurred. This, however, is credible only if St John is right in his doctrine of our Lord's person. If the Lord was indeed God incarnate, the story presents no insuperable difficulties.'

One last thing. The miracle is also a gospel 'sign', a divine action with a spiritual meaning attached to it. What is that meaning? The answer is found in the words of Jesus later in the chapter: 'I am the bread of life. Whoever comes to me shall never be hungry.' Man does not and cannot live by bread alone (O.T. lesson). Jesus himself is 'the real bread from heaven'. In him alone the lives of man are satisfied, sustained and strengthened.

FIRST SUNDAY IN LENT

Tested by the devil

St Matthew 4.1 (RSV) *'Jesus was led up by the Spirit into the wilderness to be tempted by the devil.'*

In face of the trials and testings of life nothing helps us more as Christians than the knowledge that Jesus as our brother-man has been through the same experience. Today's Epistle reminds us of this. Jesus was made like his brethren in every respect, that he might become their merciful and faithful high priest. 'For because he himself has suffered and been tempted, he is able to help those who are tempted.' As the old Scottish hymn puts it,

> In every pang that rends the heart
> The Man of Sorrows had a part.

The story of the wilderness temptation illustrates this.

The Son of God

Central to the story is the person of Jesus, who comes to the place of testing fresh from the deeply moving experience of his baptism (see previous chapter). In that crisis something tremendous had happened to him. The heavens had been rent asunder, the Spirit had descended on him, and the Father's voice had declared, 'This is my Son, my Beloved, with whom I am well pleased.' All this was in preparation for the Lord's ministry as the promised Messiah. But before he begins his ministry he must first be tested by the devil as regards his person and his mission. Hence the first temptation: 'If you are the Son of God, command these stones to become loaves of bread.' Note that *if*. The Father had said, 'This is my Son!' The devil asks, 'Are you? If so, prove it!' The temptation to Jesus here was twofold: first, to doubt his divine sonship; and second, to demonstrate it in the wrong way by ministering to his own needs, not to the needs of others. One obvious lesson emerges for us. If Jesus, the holy Son of God, was tempted by Satan, we ourselves can hardly expect to be exempt from it. Temptation is a fact of life, common to all mankind. How are we to face it?

The Spirit of God

We can discover one answer to that question by remembering that at his baptism Jesus had been anointed with the Holy Spirit. Afterwards, as St Luke puts it, he returned from the Jordan 'full of the Spirit' and was 'led by the Spirit for forty days in the wilderness'; and at the end of it all he 'returned in the power of the Spirit to Galilee'. The picture is clear. Jesus faces the experience of testing as a Spirit-filled man. So of one thing we may be sure: that to be filled with the Spirit does not mean to be free from temptation. In fact, the opposite is likely to be the case. And of another thing we may also be sure: that it is in the power of the Spirit that we too, like our Lord, shall overcome temptation, and not in our own strength.

The Word of God

Jesus won the victory in the wilderness not only by the power of the Spirit but also by the authority of the Word of God. He met each onslaught of the devil with an 'It is written!' In quoting scripture he was affirming his loyalty to the revealed will of God. The same weapon is at our disposal. In the holy war, as St Paul reminds us, we must learn to wield 'the sword of the Spirit which is the word of God'. This means that we must learn to know the Bible better and to use it skilfully. When we are tempted to do wrong, it will tell us what is right. When we are tempted to say or believe what is false, it will teach us what is true. When we are tempted to despair, it will give us assurance and hope. Bunyan was right. There is a key of Promise to unlock every door in Doubting Castle.

SECOND SUNDAY IN LENT

Deliver us from evil

> St Luke 11.14,15 (RSV) *'Jesus was casting out a demon that was dumb; when the demon had gone out, the dumb man spoke, and the people marvelled. But some of them said, "He casts out demons by Beelzebub, the prince of demons."'*

It was a terrible charge which his enemies laid against Jesus after he had healed the dumb man. They actually accused him of being in league with the devil. They did not and could not deny his supernatural power. The evidence was there before their eyes. But they attributed his power to demonic sources. 'It is by the prince of devils that he drives our devils,' they said. In this passage Jesus meets the charge and has something to say about the dark and mysterious underworld of evil which is as real an element in modern life as it was in those days long ago.

The reality of evil

Admittedly the subject of demonic possession presents us with certain difficulties and we are not as ready as those in past ages to explain every disorder in terms of evil spirits. Yet let's face it, sickness is not part of God's plan or purpose for human life. As it has been said, Jesus always regarded disease as an intruder in God's world. It represents an aspect of the evil which is inherent in the world and which takes many different forms. Jesus clearly recognised the reality of that evil and ascribed it to the powers of darkness (see Ephesians 6.12). He came into the world to do battle with those powers and to triumph over them through the cross (Colossians 2.15). The prayer he gave to his Church reaches its climax in the great cry, 'Deliver us from evil' —or as it may be rendered, 'Save us from the evil one' (NEB).

34

The activity of the devil

Well, what about the evil one? Are we content to dismiss him as a figment of the imagination or as a relic of medieval folklore? Clearly Jesus did not adopt that attitude. He spoke about the kingdom of Satan (verse 18) and described him as a strong man fully armed defending his fortress (verse 21). The picture we get here—and it is our Lord's own picture—is that of a powerful and highly organised community of evil forces at work in the world under the command of 'the prince of the power of the air'. The world itself reflects that picture. Surely it is not difficult to discern the devil's activity in the lives of people today. Indeed it is difficult to deny it. Behind so much of the fiendish wickedness present in our human situation there seems to be nothing less than satanic power which corrupts and enslaves men. There has been talk lately that God is dead. Certainly the devil is not dead. Signs of his activity are all around us.

The victory of God

Does this mean that we are to adopt a pessimistic outlook upon the world? The answer is No. While we cannot deny the reality of evil or the activity of the devil, we may be confident that the victory is with God. Jesus was manifested to destroy the works of the devil. In his earthly ministry he was far from being Satan's agent, as his enemies imputed. He was Satan's antagonist—and conqueror. The fact that demons were being cast out demonstrated that Beelzebub, prince of demons, strong though he was, had met his match and that his victims were being set free.

What of ourselves today? Do we know something of our Lord's victorious power in our lives? We may do so, if we allow him to set up his kingdom in our hearts. The little parable at the end of the Gospel warns us against the peril of an empty life. Not only must the devil be expelled: we must allow Christ to come in and reign.

THIRD SUNDAY IN LENT

The way of the cross

St Matthew 16.21 (NEB) *'From that time Jesus began to make it clear to his disciples that he had to go to Jerusalem, and there to suffer much . . . to be put to death and to be raised again on the third day.'*

To us as Christians, suffering is one of the most acute problems we have to face. Yet should it be so? For in the New Testament Christianity is closely bound up with suffering—that is, suffering for the sake of Christ and the gospel. Today's Epistle and Gospel both have a good deal to say on the subject. They point us to the suffering of Jesus as the Messiah, to the suffering of the Church as his representative in the world, and therefore to the suffering which we ourselves must be prepared to endure as his disciples.

The suffering Messiah

The gospel passage marks one of the great turning-points in our Lord's ministry. He takes his disciples apart by themselves and challenges them with some searching questions. 'What are men saying about me?' he asks. 'What is the popular opinion? And you, my disciples, what do *you* think? Who do you say I am?' These are fundamental issues. Here we are at the very heart of the gospel. The ultimate question in Christianity is, Who is Jesus? Simon Peter gave the staggering answer: 'You are the Messiah, the Son of the living God.' It was a magnificent confession of faith. And Jesus accepted it, pronouncing a blessing on Peter for this God-given insight. But immediately he went on to reveal the destiny he was to fulfil as the Messiah: he was to be rejected, to suffer and to die (see text). It was a shattering blow to the disciples. They could not and would not believe it. Peter loudly protested. A suffering Messiah! The idea seemed utterly wrong. Yet such was the Father's will; such was what the scriptures foretold; such was the path by which Jesus must accomplish his mission and redeem mankind.

36

The suffering Church

What does this mean in effect for the Church? Today's Epistle provides the answer. There Peter, who before had protested so loudly, says in effect that a suffering Christ involves a suffering Church. Suffering is as much the Church's vocation as that of its Lord. 'To that you were called,' he writes, 'because Christ suffered on your behalf, and thereby left you an example; it is for you to follow in his steps.' What the apostle is making clear here—and elsewhere in the same letter—is that the Church should not expect an easy time in a world which crucified the Lord of glory. Suffering is not something odd, surprising or exceptional but the Church's normal lot. Moreover, he makes clear that Christ's example sets the pattern for the Church: suffering must be endured patiently, bravely, trustfully (verses 22, 23).

The suffering Christian

This brings the subject down to the personal level. And here we may look at our Lord's words at the end of the Gospel: 'If anyone wishes to be a follower of mine, he must leave self behind; he must take up his cross and come with me.' To take up the cross—the words have almost lost their meaning for us today. People use the phrase about all sorts of minor trials. But in Jesus' day the man who took up his cross was on his way to execution, to die a shameful and agonising death. The symbol is a fearful one. Admittedly most of us today, at least in this country, are not called upon to suffer much for our Lord's sake. But it's worth remembering, *first*, that many of our fellow Christians in various parts of the world are suffering bitterly for their faith; *second*, that such suffering should not be regarded as an out-of-the-ordinary occurrence for the believer; and *third*, that we ourselves ought always to be ready to tread the way of the cross if the time should come.

FOURTH SUNDAY IN LENT

The glory of the Lord

St Matthew 17.1 (NEB) '*Six days later Jesus took Peter and James and John and led them up a high mountain . . .; and in their presence he was transfigured.*'

We are all familiar with serial stories in magazines and on TV in which one sequel follows another a week later. Today's Gospel is something like that. It continues the story of last Sunday's Gospel and tells what happened a week later, following Peter's great confession of Jesus as the Messiah. So we now come to the transfiguration, which marks another turning point in our Lord's ministry. Let us look at the characters involved in the story: the three chosen witnesses, the two heavenly visitors, and the one Lord in his solitary glory.

The three witnesses

Jesus took Peter, James and John with him up the mountain (Hermon). Doubtless he chose them as representatives of the twelve. We must remember that at this time the apostles were sorely perplexed by what Jesus had revealed to them a week before about his coming passion. They could not understand it. It did not fit in with their ideas about the Messiah; it seemed to deny what their scriptures foretold about his glory. To dispel their doubts and confirm their faith Jesus now took the three with him up the mountain and there revealed himself in majesty. 'In their presence he was transfigured; his face shone like the sun and his clothes became white as the light.' At that moment these men caught a vision of the glory of the Lord, in much the same way as Moses had done on Mount Sinai while he communed with God (see O.T. lesson and Epistle). For the three witnesses it was a marvellous experience. No wonder they wanted to prolong it (verse 4). Here indeed was the Messiah as they had expected to see him, invested with honour and glory (2 Peter 1.17).

The two visitors

There were two others with Jesus on the mountain beside Peter, James and John. 'They saw Moses and Elijah appear, conversing with him.' St Luke says that the two Old Testament saints 'appeared in glory' and that they 'spoke of his departure, the destiny he was to fulfil in Jerusalem'. How significant that was! In that hour of his glory the Lord was actually talking about his approaching death: the mighty redemption or liberation (literally 'exodus') he was to achieve for mankind through the cross. This was in order to convince the disciples that the cross, which had been such a stumblingblock to them before, was in harmony with the law (Moses) and the prophets (Elijah). In going up to Jerusalem to suffer and die Jesus was fulfilling the ancient scriptures and doing the Father's will. And the Father himself immediately made that clear.

The one Lord

'A bright cloud suddenly overshadowed them, and a voice called from the cloud: "This is my Son, my Beloved, on whom my favour rests; listen to him".' Peter in his confession of faith had declared, 'You are the Son of the living God!' The heavenly voice confirmed this, and added, 'Listen to him'. Peter had been reluctant to do that previously, when Jesus had spoken of his passion. 'Heaven forbid!' he had cried. Now he was learning to see the Messiah in a new light and to accept the cross as part of the divine purpose. The vision passed. The glory faded. Moses and Elijah disappeared from sight. And when the disciples raised their eyes 'they saw no one, but only Jesus'. He alone now occupied all their attention. So must it be also with us; and as with unveiled face we behold the glory of the Lord, we shall be changed into his likeness from glory to glory (see Epistle).

FIFTH SUNDAY IN LENT

Christus Victor

St John 12.20, 21 *'Among those who went up to worship at the festival were some Greeks. They came to Philip and said to him, "Sir, we would like to see Jesus".'*

The scene is set in Jerusalem. The time is the week before the Lord's passion. The men described as Greeks were Jewish proselytes who had come to worship as the passover festival. Where they had come from we do not know, nor does it matter. The point is that they were not Jews by race but Greeks, and the evangelist sees them as representatives of the Gentiles, the outside world seeking Jesus. On learning of their quest Jesus speaks about his approaching death and what it would mean to the world—the whole world, the Greeks included. As we listen to his teaching we can learn something of profound significance about the cross.

The glory of the cross

It was Philip and Andrew between them who told Jesus about the Greeks. Possibly they actually introduced them to him. At any rate on learning of their desire to see him Jesus said, 'The hour has come for the Son of Man to be glorified.' It seemed a strange response. What did he mean by his 'hour'? Undoubtedly he was referring to his death, now so near at hand. But was that the way in which he was to be 'glorified'? Most certainly! We are inclined to think of the glory of Jesus only in connection with his ascension and return to the Father. Not so St John in this gospel. He equates the glory of Jesus with the passion of Jesus. The cross is his true glory, his greatest work, his mightiest achievement. For as William Temple remarks, 'it is from the cross that the light of God's love shines forth upon the world in its fullest splendour, and Christ's death is the sealing of his victory'.

The necessity of the cross

Jesus goes on to speak to his disciples about the necessity of the cross. For this purpose he uses an illustration drawn from the world of nature. 'In truth, in very truth I tell you, a grain of wheat remains a solitary grain unless it falls into the ground and dies; but if it dies, it bears a rich harvest.' The principle he is teaching is that of life through death. If the seed is to bear fruit it must be buried in the earth and disintegrate or 'die'. When that happens it multiplies itself many times over; otherwise it remains just what it is, a single grain. In using this illustration Jesus was insisting that he must sacrifice his life to redeem mankind. The death of the One would procure life for the many. This is the essential meaning of the cross. But the same principle applies also to the Lord's followers (see verses 25, 26). In contrast to the Greek ideal of self-gratification, the servants of Jesus must follow him in the path of self-denial and self-sacrifice.

The victory of the cross

Jesus speaks of his death in terms of victory. (1) By it the Father is glorified (verses 27, 28). (2) By it the world is judged (verse 31). (3) By it the devil is defeated (verse 31). (4) By it men are converted and brought to faith (verse 32). The whole passage reaches its climax in these last great words, revealing as they do the magnetism of the cross. 'I shall draw all men to myself, when I am lifted up from the earth.' The testimony of experience proves this. What in the end conquers the hearts of men and wins them for our Lord is not his life, his example, or his teaching, powerful though these are. It is his death. The cross draws men—'all men', said Jesus. What did he mean by that? Not all men without exception, for that unhappily is not true; but all men without distinction—Greeks as well as Jews, people of every race and colour and nationality. He was referring to the universal appeal of the cross. Because of the victory he achieved by his death over sin and the law and all the cosmic powers of evil (see today's Epistle) Jesus is the Saviour of the whole world. Remember, he is your Saviour too.

PALM SUNDAY

Hosanna to the King!

St Matthew 21.9 (NEB) '*The crowd that went ahead and the others that came behind raised the shout: "Hosanna to the Son of David! Blessings on him who comes in the name of the Lord! Hosanna in the heavens!"*'

Holy week begins with the drama of our Lord's triumphal entry into Jerusalem. It is a story that readily captures the imagination and is reflected in our Palm Sunday worship. But what does it mean? All four gospels recount it, so we may be sure it has a broad general meaning for the Christian reader. But we may claim that it has a particular significance in this gospel of St Matthew; for as Charles Erdman remarks, 'Matthew is the gospel of the King; and here Jesus issues a royal command; he makes a royal progress; he receives a royal acclamation.' Here are some pegs for our thoughts today.

A royal command

'They were now nearing Jerusalem'—so the passage begins. The Lord's last great journey has reached its end. The holy city is in sight and all is set for the final conflict with the powers of evil. 'And when they reached Bethphage at the Mount of Olives Jesus sent two disciples with these instructions: "Go to the village opposite, where you will at once find a donkey tethered with her foal beside her; untie them, and bring them to me".' Jesus issues this royal command because he is about to assert and demonstrate his Messiahship. This is what Palm Sunday is really all about. The Messianic secret, hitherto concealed, is now publicly revealed—not in word but in deed. Jesus orders the donkey to be brought to him that he might deliberately fulfil the prophecy of Zechariah (see verses 4, 5).

None of the inhabitants of Jerusalem could mistake the significance of the Lord's action or evade the challenge he was presenting to them that day.

> Once to every man and nation
> Comes the moment to decide,

so wrote James Lowell, the American poet. The moment to decide came to the people of Jerusalem as Jesus presented himself to them as their promised Redeemer and King.

A royal progress

See the procession descending the Mount of Olives. Paterson Smyth describes it thus: 'In humble pageant Jesus rides in from Bethany, and his followers, as in a dream, march exultant beside him. The road is lined with crowds as for a royal procession. A shouting multitude is before him and following. Every moment the enthusiasm increases. The common road is not good enough for his progress. The Galileans are carpeting the way with their garments. The multitudes are strewing his path with green boughs and the applauding shouts are audible in Jerusalem itself . . .'

Enthusiasm! Yes, there was plenty of that. Whatever we may say about the people who joined the procession that day, they showed no lack of enthusiasm. And here surely they have something to teach us, for all too often our love is lukewarm and we show little zeal for the Lord and his kingdom. No wonder Christians have been called God's frozen people!

A royal acclamation

The enthusiastic Galileans not only spread their garments and waved their palm branches. They also raised the shout, 'Hosanna to the Son of David!' It was indeed a royal acclamation, for 'Son of David' was a kingly title. The crowd recognised in Jesus the Messiah fulfilling an ancient prophecy and they were invoking a blessing upon him. In effect they were crying, 'God save the King!'

It was as King that Jesus entered Jerusalem. That is why he was given such a rapturous welcome. But the enthusiasm soon turned to disappointment, for he had come to suffer and to die. Yet by his cross he triumphed. By death he conquered his foes, ascended to his throne, and established his kingdom. So on this Palm Sunday we too raise our loud hosannas and ascribe to him all glory, laud, and honour.

EASTER DAY

The first Easter sermon

St Mark 16.6, 7 (NEB) *'He said to them, "Fear nothing;
you are looking for Jesus of Nazareth, who was crucified.
He has risen; he is not here; look, there is the place where
they laid him. But go and give this message to his disciples
and Peter . . ."'*

Today thousands and tens of thousands of Easter sermons will
be preached in churches all over the world. The Gospel appointed for this day gives the record of the very first Easter sermon
ever to be preached and of the dramatic circumstances in which
it was preached to the women at the tomb. Let us listen to the
sermon; but first let us take a look at the preacher and the
congregation.

The preacher

Who was the preacher of the first Easter sermon? In St Matthew's
gospel he is called simply an angel. Here he is described as a
youth, wearing a white robe. Admittedly we don't know much
about angels or their ministry; but it's always well to remember
that the word *angel* means a messenger, and in the gospel records
we find angels particularly active as God's messengers in connection with the birth and resurrection of our Lord. The preacher
at the tomb is clearly such a heavenly messenger, his youthfulness
symbolising his vitality and vigour, his white robes indicating
his spotless purity.

The congregation

The first visitors to the tomb on that day were a company of
women, led by Mary Magdalene. As it has been remarked, the
practical-minded men seem to have stayed away, probably
because they had lost heart, They thought Jesus was dead, and
their faith had died with him. But the women proved that at
least their love for the Master was still alive as they made their
way to the tomb with their aromatic oils. Clearly they had no

44

expectation of seeing Jesus alive. Their purpose in coming to the tomb was simply to fulfil the final act of devotion to their crucified Lord by anointing his body. Imagine, then, their astonishment at finding the great circular stone rolled away from the entrance, and their yet greater amazement and terror on entering the tomb at being confronted with the angel-preacher in dazzling robes.

The sermon

What had the preacher to say to them? Look carefully at his message and you will find he did three things.

(1) To begin with he asserted a stupendous fact, the fact of the resurrection. 'You are looking for Jesus of Nazareth, who was crucified', he said to the women. 'He has risen, he is not here!' The announcement took the women completely by surprise. With their own eyes they had seen Jesus crucified, dead, and buried. They had come to anoint his body. Now they are told that Jesus is not dead. He has risen! Jesus is alive! This is the fact that lies at the very heart of the gospel and on which the Church is built.

(2) The preacher pointed to the evidence of the fact he had asserted—the evidence of the empty tomb. 'Look', he said, 'there is the place where they laid him'; and as he spoke he doubtless indicated the actual spot where the body of Jesus had rested. But the body was no longer there. The grave was empty because the Lord had risen. That empty grave assures us that the resurrection is a fact of history, not only a fact of experience. It is a fact which rationalism can neither explain nor explain away.

(3) What are the consequences of this fact? The first Easter sermon makes clear to us at least two of them. First, as regards ourselves: 'Fear nothing.' For the believer, all fear—and especially the fear of death—is dispelled because Jesus died and rose again. Second, as regards the world: 'Go and give this message . . .' The women were entrusted with good news for others, the good news of the living Christ. It is good news for all men. We must not keep it to ourselves. We must share it with the whole world.

FIRST SUNDAY AFTER EASTER

The difference Easter makes

> St John 20.19 (NEB) *'Late that Sunday evening, when the disciples were together behind locked doors, for fear of the Jews, Jesus came and stood among them.'*

Easter does not simply celebrate an historical fact, the fact of the resurrection and the empty tomb. It is concerned supremely with a living person, the person of the risen, all-conquering Lord. In a word, the message of Easter is not about *something* but about *Someone*. On the evening of the first Easter Sunday Jesus came and met with his disciples; and the familiar story which forms today's Gospel makes plain for all time the difference Easter makes.

The presence of Christ

'Jesus came and stood among them.' Easter makes the presence of Christ a reality. His appearance to the disciples on that Sunday evening must have caused them a good deal of astonishment. They had carefully bolted the door of the room because they were terrified of what the Jewish authorities might do to them. Such extraordinary things had happened in the course of that day. Early in the morning the tomb had been found empty and no trace of the body of Jesus could be found. Some of their number actually claimed that they had seen him—alive. We may be sure that Caiaphas and his colleagues were not a little disturbed at the course of events. They were probably threatening action against the disciples, accusing them of having stolen the body from the tomb. No wonder, when they met together that evening, the disciples took good care to lock themselves in. But no locked door can keep Jesus out; and all at once he was there, in their very midst. No doubt he had been with them all the time: now he unveiled his presence to them. And 'when the disciples saw the Lord, they were filled with joy'. His promise to them before his passion was thus fulfilled (see St John 16.22). Easter assures us that Christ is present with us always, even though now we do not see him, and his presence brings us a 'joy too great for words' (see Epistle).

The peace of Christ

The first word the Lord spoke to these anxious, frightened men was, 'Peace be with you!' Peace (*salom*) was the customary Hebrew greeting; but on the lips of the risen Christ the word now had a quite special meaning. His purpose in meeting with his disciples at that time was not simply to dispel their fears but to impart to them a quite positive gift: the gift of peace he had not only promised to them (see ch. 14.27) but which he had also so dearly purchased; for having said the greeting he 'then showed them his hands and his side'. Those wounds revealed the cost at which peace with God had been won. This is another difference Easter makes. It spells out the great word *reconciliation*. Christ made peace, and we have peace, by the blood of his cross.

The power of Christ

Easter means something more. The risen Lord not only reveals his presence to the disciples, fills them with his joy and bestows on them his peace. He also entrusts them with a commission and assures them of his power in which to fulfil it. 'As the Father sent me,' he said, 'so I send you.' Then he breathed on them, saying, 'Receive the Holy Spirit! If you forgive any man's sins, they stand forgiven; if you pronounce them unforgiven, unforgiven they remain.' These are difficult words. They raise two problems. First, was the Holy Spirit actually given then? If so, what about Pentecost? Secondly, has the Church authority to absolve sinners? In answer to those questions, the words and actions of Jesus are best regarded as a piece of prophetic symbolism. He was making clear to his disciples, then as now, that the supreme mission of the Church is to preach forgiveness of sins in his name to all nations, and that it can only fulfil that mission in the power of his promised Holy Spirit (see St Luke 24.47-49). Easter and Whitsun are here brought together in closest relationship. The one ensures the gift of pardon; the other the gift of power. Both are gifts of the living Lord Jesus.

SECOND SUNDAY AFTER EASTER

The Christ of every road

St Luke 24.15 *'Jesus himself drew near and went with them.'*

The two disciples who walked the Emmaus road that first Easter Day were, it seems, quite ordinary people. They were not apostles or anyone special. They represent the rank and file of Christians like ourselves. When they set out on their journey their minds were perplexed and their hearts were sad. But when 'Jesus himself drew near and went with them' everything was changed. The presence of the risen Lord transformed the situation and set their hearts aglow. Can the same sort of thing happen to us? The answer is Yes. For here is a picture and parable of the Christian life. The Christ of the Emmaus road is the Christ of every road. The story suggests three ways in which our communion with Christ is realised.

Through prayer

For the believer the most natural way to practise the presence of Christ is by prayer. For what is prayer? Many answers could be given; but one answer, very simple but nevertheless true, is that prayer is talking with Jesus, telling him of our difficulties and fears, sharing with him the burdens on our hearts. That is what the two disciples in our story did. They didn't ask Jesus for anything: they simply told him everything. It was so easy to speak to him. He on his part was so ready to listen. And when at length he spoke to them he showed such amazing understanding of their deepest needs. This is true prayer—opening our hearts to Christ. The best advice we can be given when in any kind of trouble is 'Tell Jesus'. Or in the words of the old mission hymn, 'Take it to the Lord in prayer.' In fellowship with him burdens are lifted, fears are dispelled, and peace is restored.

Through the scriptures

To those two disciples as he walked along the road with them the Lord 'opened the scriptures.' He answered their problem by showing them from the Old Testament that it was necessary for the Messiah both to suffer and to enter upon his glory. He 'interpreted to them in all the scriptures the things concerning himself.' It was this that made their hearts burn within them (verse 32). All at once the Bible became a new book to them. They now had the key to the book. Christ is the key that unlocks the whole of scripture, Old and New Testament alike; for within the written Word is enshrined the living Word, the Lord Jesus himself, the Word made flesh for us men and for our salvation. That is why when we read the Bible with faith and understanding we meet with Christ and enjoy fellowship with him; and our hearts too begin to glow.

Through the sacrament

At the end of that memorable walk the disciples found themselves sitting at the Lord's table; and he was 'known to them in the breaking of the bread.' It was a moment of revelation, of holy communion or *koinonia* with the living Lord. Every celebration of the Lord's supper should have the same spiritual value for us today. For the purpose of the sacrament is to make Christ real to us: the Christ who once and for all died for our sins and is now alive for evermore. We not only remember him and give thanks for the benefits of his passion. We meet with him. We feed upon him. We participate in his body and blood. Today's lesson says, 'Happy are those who are invited to the wedding supper of the Lamb!' The eucharist is a foretaste of that heavenly banquet; for as Horatius Bonar, the Presbyterian churchman and poet, wrote:

> Feast after feast thus comes and passes by;
>   Yet, passing, points to the glad feast above,
>   Giving sweet foretaste of the festal joy,
>   The Lamb's great bridal-feast of bliss and love.

THIRD SUNDAY AFTER EASTER

Joy cometh in the morning

St John 21.30 (NEB) *'Morning came, and there stood Jesus on the beach.'*

Jesus had promised his disciples that after his resurrection he would see them again in Galilee, their home country. In today's Gospel we have a revealing account of how that happened when the Lord met with them at the Sea of Tiberias. Incidentally, the appearance to the 'five hundred brethren' referred to in the Epistle probably also took place in Galilee, for this would account for the large number involved. In our story today the company was much smaller, some seven disciples in all. The miracle described is doubtless to be regarded as a 'sign', illustrating the blessing which rests on work done in obedience to the Lord's direct command.

Night: the failure of an expedition

The story begins with a disappointing night's fishing. The disciples had duly returned from Judea to Galilee and there they waited for the Lord. But Simon Peter, that restless man of action, grew tired of waiting and said to his companions one evening, 'I'm going out fishing.' The others, accustomed as they were to following his lead, agreed to accompany him. But the whole thing proved useless and futile. 'That night they caught nothing.' Break of day found them tired, jaded and disappointed after their fruitless toil. Yet their failure was hardly surprising, for the expedition on which they had set out had been self-chosen; and as Archbishop Temple remarks, 'The work which we do at the impulse of our own wills is futile.'

Daybreak: the Stranger on the beach

The fishermen were drawing near to the shore after their disappointing night's work when in the grey light of dawn they discerned a Stranger standing on the beach. He hailed them:

'Boys, have you caught anything?' Their deep sense of frustration and failure is reflected in their abrupt reply: 'No!' Then came the word of command: 'Shoot the net to starboard and you will make a catch.' Their weary state must have made them hesitate to respond; yet the authority with which the words were spoken compelled action. They cast their net as they had been instructed, with the result that they 'found they could not haul the net aboard, there were so many fish in it.' It was then that John cried out to Peter, 'It's the Lord!' And he was right. The Stranger was none other than the Lord Jesus. How did John recognise him? Perhaps by his voice. More likely by the authority with which he spoke. Most likely of all by the supernatural thing that happened. Whatever the explanation, it was just like Jesus to come to his friends in their dark hour of failure to greet them, encourage them, and satisfy their needs.

Morning: breakfast with Jesus

Having brought their catch to shore the disciples made a surprising discovery. They found a charcoal fire burning and food prepared—a most welcome sight to hungry men. Jesus gave them two directions. First, 'Bring some of your catch'; and next, when this had been done, 'Come and have breakfast.' So they sat down on the beach and had breakfast with their gracious host. Now they knew beyond a shadow of doubt who he was, their same Lord as of old, taking command of the situation and presiding at the meal. Of what did they partake? Partly of what Jesus himself had already prepared, but partly too of the fish they themselves had landed. There is a parable here, a lesson for all Christ's servants who obey his will, and it is this: we are refreshed and sustained in his service by the fruit of our own work; for in giving we ourselves receive, and faithfulness to the Lord brings its own reward.

FOURTH SUNDAY AFTER EASTER

He restoreth my soul

> St John 21.15 (RSV) '*When they had finished breakfast, Jesus said to Simon Peter, "Simon, son of John, do you love me more than these?"*'

In the previous part of this narrative the risen Lord, meeting with his disciples as promised in Galilee, dealt with them as a body, welcoming them after their night's futile fishing and preparing a meal for them on the shore. Now, when breakfast is finished, he has a special word for one of them, Simon Peter, the man who had disowned and denied him before his passion. The record of what took place between the Lord and Peter is the subject of today's Gospel and is the story of Peter's restoration.

Love challenged

Three times Jesus put to Simon the intensely personal question, 'Simon, son of John, do you love me?' In asking that he challenged his disciple's love: not only the fact of it but the depth of it. For, on the first occasion he asked the question, he added the words 'more than these'. Those words refer back to the time when, before his denial, Peter had boasted, 'Though everyone else may fall away, I will not.' In effect, Peter was then saying, 'Lord, I love you more than all these others do. They may fail you, but you can count on me. I will never let you down.' But alas, Peter's selfconfidence proved ill-founded. Three times in the garden he fell asleep. Three times in the high priest's house he denied the Lord. Surely the memory of his tragic failure must have haunted the apostle ever since! He must have longed to make restitution and to reaffirm his loyalty and devotion to his Lord. Now the opportunity was given him to do so in the presence of his colleagues. 'Simon, do you love me?' Three times the question was asked, and three times answered, to wipe out the memory of the three times Peter had so shamefully failed.

Love the test

The question the Lord put to Peter was not only a very personal one. It was also a very searching one. It went to the root of the matter. Jesus did not interrogate him about his faith or his religious opinions. His question penetrated much deeper. 'Simon, do you *love* me?' That was the test. And in the end this is the supreme test, this is what really makes a Christian. Note out Lord's judgement on the church at Laodicea (today's N.T. lesson). Outwardly that church was prosperous and no doubt highly respectable; but spiritually it was impoverished and lukewarm. It had lost its love for Jesus and had shut him out. He is seen standing at the door, knocking and asking for admission. Could that be a picture of ourselves? Orthodoxy, morality, church allegiance are not enough. The question is still, Do we love Jesus? How much does *he* mean to us?

Love in action

Another question is this. What is the proof of love? How does it show itself? In deeds, not in words. On a previous occasion Jesus had told his disciples, 'If you love me, you will keep my commandments.' So now, when Peter professed his love for the Lord, he was told, 'Feed my lambs, tend my sheep.' Clearly what Jesus was saying to Peter—and to us—was this: you must prove your love for me by showing love to others; by caring for people, young and old alike, and by ministering to their needs. Peter never forgot those words of Jesus. Later he wrote to his fellow elders: 'Tend the flock of God that is your charge, not by constraint but willingly, not for shameful gain but eagerly, not as domineering over those in your charge but being examples to the flock. And when the chief Shepherd is manifested you will obtain the unfading crown of glory' (1 Peter 5.2, 3). The Lord wants his Church to be a caring community: a community that not only professes to love him but that shows its love in action.

FIFTH SUNDAY AFTER EASTER

Plain speaking

St John 16.29 (NEB) '*His disciples said, "Why, this is plain speaking; this is no figure of speech."*'

On these Sundays after Easter we have been looking back hitherto to the resurrection narratives with their pictures of the risen Lord. In today's Gospel we look forward rather than back. We listen to Jesus speaking to his disciples about the time when his bodily presence would be withdrawn from them and he would be present with them in the Spirit. Much of what he said in his discourse puzzled them. He seemed to be using obscure 'figures of speech'. But now at the end he adopts a more direct approach and the disciples exclaim, 'Why, this is plain speaking! This is no figure of speech.' Let us listen to this plain speaking and see what we can learn from it.

About the path of prayer

'When that day comes,' says Jesus, referring to the new age of the Spirit, 'you will make your request in my name' (verse 26). He had already let them into this prayer secret when he had said, 'If you ask the Father for anything in my name, he will give it you' (verse 23). Here is plain speaking on a subject of deep importance. Prevailing prayer must be in the name of Jesus. What does that mean in practice? Not simply using the name of Jesus as a catch phrase or as a lucky charm, but praying in accordance with his mind and purpose. Prayer in the name of Christ, said William Temple, means that we pray as his representatives, as he would pray in our place, as he does pray in heaven.

About the love of God

Why may we pray with confidence to the Father in the name of the Lord Jesus? The answer is found in his words: 'The Father loves you himself, because you have loved me and believed that I came from God' (verse 27). We must never make the mistake of supposing, when we pray, that we are dealing with a reluctant heavenly Father who can only be persuaded to hear us for Christ's sake. The way to the Father is open to us all, and at all times, because his love invites and welcomes us. The love of God is the basis of everything in the Christian life. It is certainly his love that makes prayer a reality and enables us to come with boldness to the throne of grace. All that is required on our part is faith in our Lord, for we are accepted in the Beloved, and faith in God's promises, for he cannot break his word.

About the mission of the Son

Here is another matter about which Jesus speaks plainly. 'I came from the Father and have come into the world. Now I am leaving the world again and going to the Father' (verse 28). In these words Jesus speaks of the beginning and end of his earthly mission. His coming into the world refers to his birth and incarnate life; his going to the Father refers to his passion, resurrection and ascension. These are the great focal points of the gospel and of our Lord's work of redemption. He could fulfil that work only by coming into the world. The work accomplished, he returns to the Father. Dull of understanding though they are, the disciples appear to grasp this and they affirm their faith (verse 30). It was an imperfect faith as yet, but it was beginning to grow as they listened to what the Master had to say to them.

About the victory of the cross

The faith of the disciples was about to be tested. Jesus did not disguise the fact that dark times were ahead—for them as well as for him (verses 31, 32). The loneliness of the cross is in the mind of Jesus as he speaks; but he knows that the disciples will also have to tread the path of suffering. 'In the world you will have trouble,' he says. 'But courage!' he adds. 'The victory is mine; I have conquered the world.' And it was by the cross he conquered it. For him the cross was not defeat but victory. What the world thought was his shame, was his glory. We too glory in the cross; his victory is ours as well; and in him we also find peace.

Prophet, Priest and King

> St Luke 24.50 (NEB) *'Jesus led them out as far as Bethany, and blessed them with uplifted hands; and in the act of blessing he parted from them.'*

'He parted from them.' This is how St Luke describes what happened at the ascension. Jesus had parted from his friends on previous occasions during the great forty days after his resurrection. But this was something different. It was the Lord's final parting from the disciples as far as his bodily presence was concerned. Their fellowship with him in the future was to be on the spiritual level. But before he left them in this way he spoke to them as Prophet; in the act of parting he blessed them as Priest; and then he ascended to his throne as King.

The prophetic word

Jesus' final word to his men before he was parted from them was concerned with their future work and witness in the world. In the Acts Luke tells us that during the forty days he taught the disciples about the kingdom of God. Here in the gospel he spells out the teaching in greater detail. In the passage before us (verses 44–49) Jesus emphasises three things: first, that in him, crucified and risen, the messianic scriptures of the Old Testament have been fulfilled; second, that the Church was to embark upon a worldwide mission, proclaiming to all nations the good news of the forgiveness of sins in Christ's name; and third, that he would send to his people the promised gift of the Holy Spirit to clothe them with heavenly power and equip them for their service.

The priestly blessing

After leading the disciples out to Bethany, Jesus 'blessed them with uplifted hands, and in the act of blessing he parted from them'. Then returning to Jerusalem with great joy they 'spent all their time in the temple praising God'. It is significant that

Luke's gospel ends, as it began, in the temple, the place of priestly service. As one commentator has said, 'Luke's story began with a righteous priest (Zechariah) giving his blessing to the congregation of Israel. It closes with Jesus the resurrected priest giving his blessing to the messianic Israel' (E. Earle Ellis).

Jesus gave the Church his priestly blessing because his sacrificial work was completed. As the writer to the Hebrews puts it, Jesus entered the heavenly sanctuary to appear before God on man's behalf because by the shedding of his blood he had secured once for all man's eternal redemption. So it was that the last glimpse the disciples had of Jesus as he parted from them was as their High Priest:

> See! he lifts his hands above;
> See! he shows the prints of love;
> Hark! his gracious lips bestow
> Blessings on his Church below.

His kingly throne

Jesus was parted from the disciples, and as the marginal reading adds, he 'was carried up into heaven.' The language is symbolical, indicating that he was exalted to his throne. 'To him was given dominion and glory and kingdom, that all peoples, nations and languages should serve him,' as Daniel's great vision describes it in today's Old Testament reading. And St Paul in the Epistle uses the same sort of majestic language when he refers to the power which God 'exerted in Christ when he raised him from the dead, when he enthroned him at his right hand in the heavenly realms, far above all government and authority, all power and dominion . . .' The message of the ascension is 'Jesus is Lord'. The throne of the universe is his. He is supreme head of the Church. It is for us to acknowledge his sovereignty over our own lives, and then to work for the furtherance of his kingly rule in all the world.

WHITSUNDAY

The Spirit of Christ

St John 14.16–18 (RSV) *'I will pray the Father, and he will give you another Counsellor, to be with you for ever, even the Spirit of truth ... I will not leave you desolate; I will come to you.'*

Whitsunday celebrates the coming of the Holy Spirit on the day of Pentecost to abide with the Church for ever. We all know that. But who is this Holy Spirit who then came? How are we to think of him? And what does his coming signify? Perhaps the most important thing is to think of the Holy Spirit in direct relationship to the Lord Jesus himself: to think of him in other words as the Spirit of Christ. We are on solid biblical ground when we do that. Therefore on this Whitsunday we shall be wise to view the historical event described in the second chapter of Acts in the light of our Lord's teaching in today's Gospel.

The Holy Spirit is the gift of Christ

The Holy Spirit is, as the hymn puts it, the 'great gift of our ascended King'. He is Christ's own birthday gift to his people for all time. He came in response to Christ's prayer: 'I will ask the Father, and he will give you another to be your Advocate' (NEB). And on the day of Pentecost the apostle Peter declared, as he preached about Jesus: 'Being exalted at the right hand of God, and having received from the Father the promise of the Holy Spirit, he has poured out this which you see and hear' (Acts 2.33). It was all Christ's doing. He prayed the Father; he received the promised gift; he bestowed the Spirit. Here is the culmination of our Lord's work for his Church. He gives the Spirit as the seal of the redemption he has wrought.

The Holy Spirit is Christ in us

The Holy Spirit is not only Christ's gift to us. In a deep and true sense he is Christ in us. 'I will not leave you bereft,' he promised; 'I am coming back to you.' And he came back to them at Pentecost in the person of the Holy Spirit. When the Spirit came that day it must have seemed to the disciples that the Lord Jesus was with them again; and so he was. 'Lo, I am with you always' he assured them before his ascension. Moreover, by this means he was with them all, with them in every place, with them for ever; for as it has been wisely said, the Holy Spirit was given not to compensate for Christ's absence, but to ensure Christ's presence.

This is how we should think of the Holy Spirit, in closest association with Christ himself. He is in a real sense Jesus' 'other self', dwelling in our hearts, imparting to us his presence, peace and power. The healthy-minded Christian is not always thinking and talking about the Holy Spirit. He is occupied with Christ, for Christ is the centre of his faith. It is the office of the Spirit to glorify Christ and make him real. So we can make this final statement.

The Holy Spirit is the interpreter of Christ

Look at these words at the end of the Gospel: 'I have told you all this while I am still here with you; but your Advocate, the Holy Spirit whom the Father will send in my name, will teach you everything, and will call to mind all that I have told you' (NEB). There was much that the disciples could not understand about Jesus during his earthly life—and he recognised that. So he assured them that after he had left them the Holy Spirit, the Spirit of truth, would be their teacher and enlighten their minds and make everything clear to them. This is what we mean when we say that the Holy Spirit is the interpreter of Christ. He guides us into all truth. He takes of the things of Christ and declares them to us, especially the things recorded in holy scripture.

If then we ask again the question, Who is the Holy Spirit? the answer is, He is the Spirit of Christ: Christ's gift to us, Christ's presence with us, Christ's mind revealed in us.

TRINITY SUNDAY

Worship

Isaiah 6.1–3 (RSV) '*I saw the Lord sitting upon a throne, high and lifted up; and his train filled the temple. Above him stood the seraphim; . . . and one called to another and said:*

> "*Holy, holy, holy is the Lord of hosts; the whole earth is full of his glory.*" '

Trinity Sunday confronts us with the fact of God, God in his essential being. In the light of the revelation of his nature which we have celebrated in the previous part of the Christian year we are now given grace, as the collect puts it, 'to acknowledge the glory of the eternal Trinity, and in the power of the divine Majesty to worship the Unity'. Worship then is a proper subject for our consideration today; and it may be well to face the question, What is worship? The scripture readings appointed will help us as we seek to find the answer.

Worship is an obligation

The first thing to be said is that worship is an obligation. It is a duty, not an option. It is something we owe to God. The very word reminds us of that, for worship is man's recognition of the 'worthship' of God. It is his attempt, however feeble and unworthy, to give to the Lord the glory due to him as Creator and Redeemer. This is what St Paul is doing in today's Epistle when he cries, 'Praise be to the God and Father of our Lord Jesus Christ, who has bestowed on us in Christ every spiritual blessing in the heavenly realms!' The whole passage is in fact a great act of worship. Such worship is not only an obligation: it is our *primary* obligation. The ten commandments make that clear, for the very first of them is a call to worship the only true and living God (Exodus 20.2, 3). And Jesus endorsed this when he affirmed that the thing that matters most in religion is that we should love the Lord our God with all the powers we possess. Such adoration finds its outward expression in worship.

Worship is an activity

Worship is not only something we owe. It is also something we do, something in which we are directly involved. If we think of worship in terms of drama, then we are present not as members of the audience, looking on, but as members of the cast, taking part. Each worshipper is required to be a participant, not a spectator. Penitence, prayer, intercession, praise, thanksgiving, hearing God's word, confessing our faith: these are the ingredients of worship and they are all activities of the soul of man. The Old Testament lesson illustrates this. The prophet Isaiah is worshipping in the temple at Jerusalem when he is caught up in the adoration of the heavenly host and glimpses a vision of the holiness of God. As a result he bows in contrition before the Lord, acknowledges his sin, receives assurance of divine forgiveness, hears the word of God, and offers his life in an act of dedication.

Worship is a response

How is it possible for man to engage in this activity of worship? Because God in his grace has revealed himself to man, not only in word but in deed. Worship is a response to that revelation. It is impossible to worship an unknown God (Acts 17.23). Clearly worship and revelation are bound up together. We worship God aright only in so far as we know God; and we know God only in so far as he reveals himself to us. That is why on this Trinity Sunday we worship God in his triune majesty as Father, Son, and Holy Spirit—because God has been pleased to disclose himself to us as such in scripture, and supremely in the Word made flesh. So in today's Gospel we hear our Lord saying to us, as to his disciples of old, 'If you knew me, you would know my Father too... Anyone who has seen me has seen the Father.... I am in the Father and the Father in me.' God has spoken to us through his Son, who is the image of the invisible God; and in response to that revelation we are enabled to worship him, not only with the heart but with the understanding, both in spirit and in truth.

FIRST SUNDAY AFTER TRINITY

The Church

1 Peter 2.9 (RSV) '*You are a chosen race, a royal priesthood, a holy nation, God's own people, that you may declare the wonderful deeds of him who called you out of darkness into his marvellous light.*'

The story is told of an American business man who applied to his minister to join the church. 'I would like to become a member of the firm', he said, using his business jargon, 'but I don't want anybody to know it. I would like to come into the concern as a sleeping partner.' The minister's answer was: 'Jesus Christ takes no partners on those terms. The name of the firm is "Jesus Christ and Company", and the names of the company must all be written out on the signboard for the world to read.' The Church is indeed Jesus Christ and company, a company of people in union with him, as the branch is in union with the vine (see Gospel). Today's Epistle gives us some other pictures of the Church.

The family of God

The opening verses speak of Christians as 'twice-born' people who by faith and baptism have been made children of God. This means that the Church is God's family, a fact which we recognise every time we repeat the Lord's prayer and say, 'Our Father in heaven'. The fatherhood of God is bound up with the family of God. Because *he* is our Father, *we* are his children. What sort of children should we be? The apostle says we should be healthy, thriving children, nourished on 'pure milk', the milk of spiritual truth, and so 'grow up to salvation'. The call to us here is to become more holy, to deepen our knowledge of God, to feed on his word. What is your spiritual appetite like nowadays?

The temple of God

At verse 4 the figure abruptly changes and the apostle introduces a new image. Christians are now described as 'living stones', built into a 'spiritual house'—that is, the Church of which Christ himself is the precious cornerstone. Then the figure is modified further; for believers are seen not only as the stones which make up the fabric of this holy temple but as a 'holy priesthood' exercising their ministry within it and offering up 'spiritual sacrifices acceptable to God through Jesus Christ'. It is a marvellous picture of the Church in its priestly capacity and as a worshipping community. Note that the priesthood belongs to the whole Church, to all believers. The call now is to rejoice in the privilege that is ours, of access to God through Christ, our great High Priest, and to draw near to him in fellowship one with another; to offer up our sacrifices of praise and thanksgiving, of our alms and gifts, and above all of our lives in his service.

The Israel of God

In the last part of the passage the picture changes again. Now the Church is seen as 'the Israel of God' (Galatians 6.16), that is as the new People of God, members of the new covenant. 'You are a chosen race, a royal priesthood, a holy nation, God's own people.' The titles are all taken from the Old Testament, largely from our lesson in Exodus 19. Those titles are now applied to the new redeemed community. What was ideally true of the People of Israel of old is now actually true of the People of Christ. Christians *are* God's elect, a kingdom of priests, a people set apart for his possession and service. And what is their function? To 'declare the wonderful deeds of him who called us out of darkness into his marvellous light'. So the final challenge to us today has to do with our Christian witness. The Church is here in the world to make known the good news, to tell of what God has done for men in Christ. And this involves us all. Remember, the Church is Jesus Christ and company—and *you* are a member of the company.

SECOND SUNDAY AFTER TRINITY

Baptised into Christ

Romans 6.3,4 (RSV) *'Do you not know that all of us who have been baptised into Christ Jesus were baptised into his death? We were buried therefore with him by baptism into death, so that as Christ was raised from the dead by the glory of the Father, we too might walk in newness of life.'*

It has been said that Christianity is not a label but a life. It is easy enough to wear the label, to profess and call ourselves Christians just because we have been baptised; it is much more difficult to live the life. Yet that is the real test. What sort of life is required of us? The apostle says that the very label we wear, baptism itself, provides the pattern. Far from being a mere formality, baptism makes very definite demands upon us and shows us the kind of people we should be: dead with Christ to sin, risen with Christ to righteousness, and walking with Christ in newness of life.

Dead with Christ to sin

The apostle is here answering a question: 'Are we to continue in sin that grace may abound?' This was how some of the enemies of the gospel argued. They said in effect, 'Since we are saved by grace, then the more we sin the more we magnify God's grace. So let's persist in sin that his grace may abound yet more'. The apostle's answer is emphatic. 'God forbid!' he says. 'We died to sin: how can we live any longer in it? Have you forgotten that when you were baptised into Christ you were baptised into his death?' As a sacramental or symbolical rite baptism is regarded as a sort of death and burial (in the early church it was commonly administered by immersion). It therefore portrays our being crucified, dead, and buried with Christ and requires us to say accordingly, 'I renounce evil.' This is the negative side of the baptised life. But there is a positive side as well.

Risen with Christ to righteousness

Baptism speaks of resurrection as well as of death. We must picture the scene St Paul has in mind at the river-side. The candidate for baptism enters the water, goes beneath it to bury his sins in Christ's grave, and then emerges from it to rise with Christ to a life finished with sin. The apostle uses strong language in this passage to describe the new quality of holiness that should be ours if we are truly risen with Christ (verses 5-11). Crucified and risen with him, we are no longer the slaves of sin. We now serve a new Master who has conquered death and sin and leads us in the way of his triumph. The idea of deliverance from the slavery of sin is illustrated in the Old Testament lesson (Deuteronomy 6.21-23). The meaning of union with Christ is illustrated in the Gospel (John 15.6).

Walking with Christ in newness of life

This is the continuing process of the risen life. Christ was raised from the dead by the glory of the Father, says St Paul, that 'we too might walk in newness of life'. *Walking* is one of his favourite metaphors of the Christian life. It speaks of that life in terms of pilgrimage: the steady going on with Christ day by day, growing in the knowledge of him, facing and over-coming temptation in his strength, bearing fruit in his service, abiding in his love, pressing on towards the heavenly goal. Our baptism commits us to this new quality of discipleship and calls us to tread the way of holiness as those who are 'alive to God in Christ Jesus' (verse 11).

To be 'in Christ' is to be in union with him. This is the key to today's Epistle. It is the key to the meaning of baptism. It is also the key to the new life which is ours now as we share with Christ not only in his death and burial but also in his resurrection victory and the power of his endless life.

THIRD SUNDAY AFTER TRINITY

Free in Christ

Galatians 4.7 (NEB) '*You are therefore no longer a slave but a son and if a son, then also by God's own act an heir.*'

The passage which forms today's Epistle is by no means easy. But the message it conveys is perfectly clear and that message is summed up in these final words. St Paul is urging the Galatians, who had already abandoned the old slavery of paganism, to renounce the new slavery of legalism which was threatening to imprison them, and to rise to their exalted status in Christ as sons of God. Moreover, he reminds them that they are grown-up sons, not just children, and that as such they have reached a stage of spiritual maturity and spiritual freedom as heirs of God's riches. This is the gist of the apostle's teaching. It is worth looking at in a little more detail.

Man come of age

One of the phrases often bandied about nowadays is that of 'man come of age'. It is sometimes used without much under-standing, and sometimes in a quite unbiblical way. But the phrase does embody a deep spiritual truth, a truth which St Paul expounds here. He uses an illustration about a boy who is the son of a rich father. The father has died, leaving him all his wealth but stipulating the age at which his son is to inherit. Until he reaches that age the boy cannot touch his father's money. He is subject to those who manage his father's estate and is no better than a servant. But once he reaches the appointed age he enters upon his inheritance: he is free from his guardians, he possesses his promised wealth, he is able to exercise the full privilege of sonship. So, says the apostle, it is with Christian believers. They have left behind their religious childhood. Spiritually speaking they have come of age, they are God's sons and heirs, they are free.

Christ the Liberator

How did it happen? The answer is that at a certain point in time, after a long period of preparation, God took decisive action for man's salvation. 'When the term was completed, God sent his own Son, born of a woman, born under the law, to purchase freedom for the subjects of the law, in order that we might attain the status of sons.' The epoch of man's bondage under the Mosaic law (Judaism) and under what Paul calls 'the elemental spirits of the universe' (paganism) ended with the coming of Christ. His purpose in coming into the world was to end the reign of law and to break the tyranny of sin, so that by his grace we might enjoy the freedom of the sons of God. It is none of our doing. Christ is the Liberator. Through him we are set free, adopted into God's family, and made inheritors of his kingdom.

The witness of the Spirit

This is a marvellous position! Can we be sure of it? Yes, says the apostle: 'To prove that you are sons, God has sent into our hearts the Spirit of his Son, crying "Abba! Father!"' The argument now is based on Christian experience. God has not only sent his Son into the world; he has also sent his Spirit into our hearts. The great objective work of redemption wrought in time and history by the passion of our Lord is accompanied by the interior subjective work of the Holy Spirit crying out within us 'Father!' as we come to God in prayer. That word signifies the new relationship we have with God in Christ. It is a word which a slave could never use in addressing his master. But it is the word we use spontaneously in our approach to God; and this indicates, as the apostle says, that our position is no longer that of a slave but that of a son. And more still: 'if a son, then also by God's own act an heir'—put into the possession of all the spiritual riches God has to give to his sons.

FOURTH SUNDAY AFTER TRINITY

The law of Christ

Ephesians 5.2, 8 (RSV) *'Walk in love, as Christ loved us and gave himself up for us . . . Walk as children of light.'*

Last Sunday's theme was the freedom of the sons of God. That subject at once raises an important issue for us as Christians. In what sense are we 'free'? Are we free to do what we like? Are we free from the law? For example, are we free to ignore the ten commandments, which form today's Old Testament lesson? These are questions we ought to think about in the light of the New Testament.

Law

The first thing to be said is that Christianity is not a legalistic religion. Christians are not subject to the Jewish or any other code of law. As St John puts it, 'The law was given through Moses; grace and truth came through Jesus Christ'; and St Paul declares plainly that as Christians we are 'not under law but under grace'. The rest of the New Testament is in agreement with this. In one sense, then, we *are* free from the law—free from the law as a way of salvation. None of us by obedience to God's commands can merit forgiveness of sins or purchase a place in heaven. Salvation is all of grace, not of works. But while that is true, we are *not* free from the law (the moral law) as a way of life. Christianity is not a sort of 'go-as-you-please' affair. Just because we love God we desire to please him, not ourselves, and to follow the pattern of life laid down in the Bible as a whole, and especially in the ethical teaching given by Jesus and his apostles in the New Testament.

Love

This means that the concept of law has a place in the Christian faith. Indeed, St Paul twice speaks about the 'law of Christ' (1 Corinthians 9.21; Galatians 6.2). What is that law? The answer is that it is not an external, complicated set of rules but rather a single inner principle—the principle of *love*. And so we come to the apostle Paul's words at the beginning of today's Epistle: 'be imitators of God, as beloved children. And walk in love, as Christ loved us and gave himself up for us, a fragrant offering and sacrifice to God.' Note how high a standard the apostle sets before us. We are to be imitators of *God*: not of men, not even of saints and angels. God is love, and we are his children; as such we are to reproduce the family likeness and to 'walk in love'. St Paul is not being sentimental when he says that. The love of which he speaks is something very costly. He points us to the cross, to the love of Christ in dying for us sinners, and he declares that that love is to be at once the model, the measure, and the motive of our own love. To walk in love is to live unselfishly, sacrifically, and to interpret the whole of life in terms of service. This is the law of Christ, the law by which he lived—and died.

Light

It is noteworthy that the apostle exhorts us not only to walk in love but to 'walk as children of light'. Why is this? Because God is light as well as love. His love is a holy thing, and if we are to imitate him we too must be holy. The 'fruit of light', says St Paul—that is, the fruit that grows in the light of God's love— 'is found in all that is good and right and true'. On the other hand we must shun 'the unfruitful works of darkness', and those works are made quite clear in verses 3–5: sexual impurity, filthy talk, coarse jesting, the idolatrous worship of material things. We talk about our permissive age. The days in which Paul wrote were just as permissive. It couldn't have been easy for the first century Christians he was addressing to turn their backs on the old pagan way of life and to be 'different'; yet that is what was demanded of them. The same demand is made on us today. Those who accept the law of Christ must not only place themselves under the rule of love. They must also observe a perpetual festival of light.

FIFTH SUNDAY AFTER TRINITY

The new life in Christ

Colossians 3.17 (RSV) *'Whatever you do, in word or deed, do everything in the name of the Lord Jesus, giving thanks to God the Father through him.'*

Today's Epistle indicates very clearly the quality of the new life demanded of us as Christians. But more than that: not only does the brief passage describe the sort of people we should be. It also lets us into the secret as to how we can be that sort of people. The clue to it all is Christ. The apostle's urgent exhortations throughout the passage find their centre in him. He tells us that our relationships must be motivated by Christ's forgiveness, our hearts ruled by Christ's peace, our minds enriched by Christ's word, and our conduct regulated by Christ's name.

The forgiveness of Christ

'As the Lord has forgiven you, so you also must forgive' (verse 13). Here at the beginning of the passage St Paul is dealing with the delicate matter of personal relationships. He calls upon his readers to clothe themselves with compassion, humility, patience, and forbearance. This, as he knows well, will mean exercising a forgiving spirit; and he knows equally well how difficult in practice that is. How can we forgive others? The answer is: by recalling Christ's forgiveness of us. In that great act of divine grace, so wonderfully illustrated in the story of the prodigal son (Gospel), we find the motive power to be charitable and forbearing to those who have wronged us. We forgive, because we have been forgiven. In this Christ is not only our Saviour: he is also our example.

The peace of Christ

'Let the peace of Christ rule in your hearts' (verse 15). The word rendered *rule* is interesting. It means literally to arbitrate, and so the NEB version is, 'Let Christ's peace be arbiter in your hearts.' The task of an arbitrator is to decide all matters of difference, to sort out the right from the wrong. So it must be with Christ's peace within us. Anything that disturbs our possession of that peace is to be rejected as sinful and wrong. As Bishop Lightfoot expressed it: 'Whenever there is a conflict of motives or impulses or reasons, the peace of Christ must step in and decide which is to prevail.'

The word of Christ

'Let the word of Christ dwell in you richly, as you teach and admonish one another in all wisdom' (verse 16). Just as our hearts are to be ruled by Christ's peace, so our minds are to enriched by his word or 'message' (NEB). We get here a little picture of the instructed Christian, learning more about Christ's teaching as he shares the life of corporate discipleship and joins in the worship of the church (see remainder of verse). It should be a picture of us all. One thing we quickly discover when we study the word of Christ: how timeless his teaching is and how relevant it is to the world of our day. He has much to say to us on such issues as marriage and divorce, the use of money, social responsibility, family life, and so on.

The name of Christ

Christ's teaching is not simply to be studied. It is to be obeyed; and so the apostle says our conduct must be regulated by his name. 'Whatever you do, in word or deed, do all in the name of the Lord Jesus, giving thanks to God the Father through him' (verse 17). Perhaps there is a warning here, that there are some things we cannot do with a good conscience in Christ's name, and that such things are to be shunned. But the positive side is unmistakably clear, that the honour of our Lord should be the aim and object of all we say and do and that our daily conduct should be a good advertisement for him.

SIXTH SUNDAY AFTER TRINITY

In praise of love

> 1 Corinthians 13.13 (NEB) '*The greatest of them all is love.*'

St Paul was a man of many parts. We think of him as scholar and theologian, author and preacher, missionary pioneer and church administrator. Seldom do we think of him as poet; yet it was he who gave us the marvellous hymn in praise of *agape* or love which forms today's Epistle and which is undoubtedly one of the finest poems ever written. As we consider the familiar words again let us try to discover in them some fresh meaning for ourselves.

Love is the greatest

Over sixty years ago Professor Henry Drummond, the Scottish scientist, published his little book called *The Greatest Thing in the World*. The substance of it was an address given to students of Edinburgh University, based on this 13th chapter of 1 Corinthians. Drummond's purpose was to show that Christian love is the *summum bonum*, the supreme good—indeed, the ultimate secret of life. St Paul had fully grasped that secret, and here at the beginning of his poem he exalts love to the highest level by showing that without it all other gifts are useless. He lists some of these gifts, particularly those which were coveted by the Corinthians: eloquence, prophecy, knowledge, faith, generosity self-sacrifice; and he says in effect, If I have all these and yet have no love, I am worth nothing at all. At the end of the poem he puts love alongside faith and hope as forming a holy trio; but without hesitation he affirms, 'The greatest of them all is love.' Yes, love is the greatest. Jesus said the same: love is the first commandment and the fulfilling of all the commandments. The fact is, love is supreme because love is divine; for as St John wrote, 'God is love; and he who dwells in love dwells in God, and God in him.'

Love has a human face

Because 'God is love' we may be sure that love is not impersonal. It is hardly surprising therefore that in the middle of his poem the apostle personifies love. He does not simply describe it. He portrays it. He paints a picture in words. 'Love is patient; love is kind and envies no one. Love is never boastful, nor conceited, nor rude; never selfish, not quick to take offence. Love keeps no score of wrongs; does not gloat over other men's sins, but delights in the truth. There is nothing love cannot face; there is no limit to its faith, its hope, and its endurance.'

The picture is perfectly clear; and if we ask, Whose portrait is this? the answer must be, in the words of Peter of old, 'It is the Lord!' Love has a human face, the face of Jesus. In him we see exemplified the features set out here: patience, kindness, humility, unselfishness, endurance, and all the rest. Clearly love is not an emotion or a sentiment. It is a character, it is likeness to Christ. And to 'follow after love' is to walk in the steps of the Lord Jesus himself.

Love endures for ever

Love is supreme. Love is personal. And love is also eternal: 'Love will never come to an end.' This is the final theme of Paul's poem as he dwells upon the permanence of love. Other things are of a temporary nature, fleeting and fading. Love lasts for ever. Prophetic utterances, tongues of ecstasy, all stores of human knowledge—these will pass away. In the end there are but three things that endure: faith, hope, and love; but of these, declares the apostle, one reigns supreme, and he brings forth the crown and places it on the head of love. So, he adds, 'Put love first' (ch. 14.1)—for love has eternal value. Cultivate it. Practise it. Live it. For as Henry Drummond declared in his lecture, 'To love abundantly is to live abundantly, and to love for ever is to live for ever.'

SEVENTH SUNDAY AFTER TRINITY

Life in the Spirit

> Galatians 5.22, 23 (RSV) *'The fruit of the Spirit is love, joy, peace, patience, kindness, goodness, faithfulness, gentleness, self-control.'*

In today's Gospel we hear our Lord saying to his disciples, 'You did not choose me, but I chose you and appointed you that you should go and bear fruit and that your fruit should abide' (St John 15.16). In the Epistle St Paul tells us what that fruit is, the fruit that abides. He calls it the fruit of the Spirit, setting it in opposition to the works of the flesh; and he urges us so to allow the Holy Spirit to take control of our lives that the lusts of the flesh may be put to death and we may be fashioned more and more in the likeness of Jesus Christ. Here are things worth thinking about today.

Flesh and Spirit

Let us begin by noting the contrast between the two levels of life which the apostle sets before us as stark alternatives. The one level is that of the flesh, by which he means our 'lower nature', as the NEB has it: the level of our fallen and sinful humanity which we inherit at birth. 'That which is born of the flesh is flesh', as Jesus said. But he also said, 'That which is born of the Spirit is spirit'; and so another level of life is possible for us, life in the Spirit as the result of our new supernatural birth. These two levels of life are in direct conflict with one another. Our fleshly nature is pulling in one direction, our spiritual nature in the other. We cannot go in both directions at once. What then are we to do? Here is the answer: 'Walk by the Spirit, and do not gratify the desires of the flesh'; and again, 'If you are led by the Spirit you are not under the law' (verses 16, 18). The man whose life is surrendered to the Spirit finds release both from the bondage of the flesh and from the burden of the law.

Works and fruit

Let us next look at two other words which stand in opposition. The apostle goes on to speak of the *works* of the flesh and the *fruit* of the Spirit. (Unfortunately the NEB obscures this contrast.) The works of the flesh listed (verses 19–21) have been classified as sexual sins (immorality, impurity, licentiousness); pagan sins (idolatry, sorcery); sins of faction (enmity, strife, jealousy, anger, selfishness, dissension, party spirit, envy); and sins of appetite (drunkenness, carousing). These ugly things are 'works' because they are our own doing, the result of our self-indulgence and sinful passions. On the other hand the list of virtues which follows is called the 'fruit' of the Spirit because they are not our own product but the natural growth of the indwelling Spirit of God. What lovely things they are! 'Love, joy, peace, patience, kindness, goodness, faithfulness, gentleness, selfcontrol.' It is by this kind of character, this likeness to Christ himself, that the believer is to be recognised and identified; for as the Lord himself said, a tree is known by its fruit. It cannot be emphasised too strongly today that the real evidence that we 'belong to Christ Jesus' (verse 24) is not that we exercise the gifts of the Spirit but that we bear the fruit of the Spirit. Character counts for more than achievement.

Living and walking

The application comes in the closing words: 'If we live by the Spirit, let us also walk by the Spirit.' By that the apostle simply means that just as the Spirit is the source of our new regenerate life in Christ, so he must order and direct our daily 'walk' in the world. 'Being "in the Spirit" is not just an inner experience. It is something that has to be translated into action, and to be our guide in every relationship of life' (Stephen Neill). This is the personal challenge of today's Epistle. This is the practical outcome of the Spirit-filled life.

EIGHTH SUNDAY AFTER TRINITY

Church militant

> Ephesians 6.10, 11 (NEB) *'Find your strength in the Lord, in his mighty power. Put on all the armour which God provides, so that you may be able to stand firm against the devices of the devil.'*

With the virtual disappearance of the Book of Common Prayer from our worship one of its most striking phrases is now dropping out of use: 'the Church militant here in earth'. The value of the phrase is that it reminds us of an important aspect of the Church's life. Christianity is not a spiritual picnic or a sort of Pleasant Sunday Afternoon religion. It is a battle royal against the world, the flesh, and the devil. That is why in the passage before us the apostle depicts the Church as the army of God, equipped for the holy war.

The holy war

Let us think about this holy war and take note of the kind of enemy we are up against. St Paul's description is a vivid one. 'Our fight', he says, 'is not against human foes, but against cosmic powers, against the authorities and potentates of this dark world, against the superhuman forces of evil in the heavens.' The point the apostle is making here is that the Church's battle is a spiritual one. Our foes are not human, not 'flesh and blood', but 'the superhuman forces of evil in the heavens'. This makes the struggle none the less real, and certainly none the less easy. As Christians we are engaged in a real war, against a real enemy. We must be blind indeed if we do not recognise the reality of the evil forces at work around us today, in the world and in the lives of men. As members of the Church militant we are called upon to fight on many fronts: for example, in the battle for the truth of the gospel in an age of false ideologies; in the battle for religious and political freedom in an age of tyranny; in the battle for Christian moral standards in an age of obscenity; above all, in the battle for world evangelisation in an age of deepening spiritual darkness.

The weapons of our warfare

The Lord not only calls us to engage in this warfare of the spirit. He also equips us for the fight. So St Paul urges us, 'Put on all the armour which God provides', and he proceeds to describe what this armour is in terms of the warfare of his day. He mentions six or seven bits of equipment: the belt of truth, the breastplate of righteousness, the shoes of the gospel, the shield of faith, the helmet of salvation, the sword of God's word, and the weapon of 'all-prayer', as Bunyan called it. The figures of speech may be out of date, but the facts they represent are living and abiding. What Paul is saying to us in our fight against evil is something like this:

> Be loyal to your deepest convictions.
> See that your life is marked by absolute integrity.
> Take your stand firmly on the reconciling gospel.
> Put you whole trust in the Lord.
> Claim continually the saving power of Christ.
> Attack the enemy with the inspired scriptures.
> Keep in close touch with God always.

The call to arms

What then? We must go into action. We must heed the call to arms. In fact a threefold call sounds out to us in this passage. *First*, 'Find your strength in the Lord, in his might power'—not in your own feeble efforts, in purely human resources. *Second*, 'Put on all the armour which God provides.' The arm of flesh will fail us; God's armour alone is adequate. That armour is ready to hand. We do not have to provide it, but we do have to wear it—all of it, for each piece is important. *Third*, 'Stand firm' —that is, maintain your ground, even when things are at their worst. Do not retreat or shirk the fight but face the enemy in the name of the Lord. Such a church militant will also be a church triumphant, even here in earth.

NINTH SUNDAY AFTER TRINITY

The mind of Christ

> Philippians 2.5 (RV) *'Have this mind in you, which was also in Christ Jesus.'*

Factions in church life are all too common, even in the best congregations, as we would all sadly admit. It may be some slight consolation to know that such things were not unheard of in apostolic times. The Church at Philippi was a case in point. There was among its members a tendency to dissension and party spirit, as this letter makes quite clear; and one of St Paul's objects in writing is to appeal to them to be united in love, to cultivate a humble self-forgetting spirit, to consider one another's interests, not their own. What argument can he bring forward to reinforce his plea? He uses the highest argument of all by pointing them to the example of Christ himself when he came to earth from heaven to save mankind. The result is this marvellous Hymn of the Incarnation on which we are asked to reflect today, so that we may know the mind of Christ and learn the secret of true fellowship.

His divine glory

The hymn begins and ends in eternity. Its sweep is quite literally 'from glory to glory': from heaven's throne to Calvary's cross, and from the cross back to the throne. To make his point clear, the apostle begins by asserting Christ's divine pre-existence, before time was, before the world was made. 'He subsisted in the form of God'—an expression which indicates that from the first he possessed the very nature and attributes of God. In all essentials he was one with the Father, co-equal and co-eternal; for 'in the beginning was the Word, and the Word was with God, and the Word was God'. Such was the everlasting glory of God the Son.

His self-emptying

But what did he do? Though the divine nature was thus his, he 'did not count equality with God a thing to be grasped, but emptied himself, taking the form of a servant, being born in the likeness of men'. It is to this supreme example of the Lord's self-emptying, his humiliation in becoming truly man and servant of others, that St Paul particularly directs his quarrelsome readers at Philippi. He is urging them to abandon their pride, to give up all big ideas of themselves, and so to love and serve one another. Why? Because this was the mind of Christ, who stripped himself of his glory to be born as man and fulfil the servant's role. And more than that: 'being found in human form he humbled himself and became obedient unto death, even death on a cross'.

Today's Gospel illustrates the truth the apostle is setting forth here. On the night before he died Jesus said to his disciples, 'I am among you as one who serves'; and then he suited his actions to his words by laying aside his garments, girding himself with a towel, pouring water into a basin, and washing the disciples' feet. In this way he literally 'took the form of a servant', for feet-washing was a slave's task; and having done so he told the disciples, 'I have set you an example: you are to do as I have done for you.' Such is the mind of Christ—the attitude of self-forgetting love expressing itself in lowly service.

His exaltation

The apostle might have ended his hymn at the point we have so far reached, for his illustration is now complete. But he cannot leave the Lord on the cross, so he adds this magnificent coda:

'Therefore God raised him to the heights
    and bestowed on him the name above all names,
that at the name of Jesus every knee should bow—
    in heaven, on earth, and in the depths—
and every tongue confess, "Jesus Christ is Lord",
    to the glory of God the Father.'

It has been said that Christ twice passed the angels by. He was made lower than them in his incarnation; he was raised far above them in his exaltation. The hymn as a whole is at once an act of worship and a confession of faith, bearing witness to Christ:

his eternal pre-existence, his human birth, his life of service, his shameful death, his glorification, his adoration by men and angels, his lordship over all creation. Wonderful! Yet we must not let the wonder of it blind us to the apostle's entirely practical purpose in quoting these words. He is directing our attention to the Lord Jesus Christ not for our admiration but for our emulation. He want us to see in him the perfect pattern of love, humility and service; and he says to us, 'Have this mind in *you*, which was also in Christ Jesus.'

TENTH SUNDAY AFTER TRINITY

Service for Christ

2 Corinthians 4.1 (RSV) *'Having this ministry by the mercy of God, we do not lose heart.'*

The leader of one of the small Christian communities on the Continent was once asked, 'How many members have you in your church?' He gave the figure: 'Such and such a number.' 'And now many ministers have you in your church?' he was next asked. The triumphant answer came back, 'The same number! In our church all members are ministers of Christ.' He meant that all members had a sense of vocation and formed a serving community. So should it be with us. 'We have this ministry', says St Paul. How are we to fulfil it? From the passage we can gather some general principles of Christian service.

We serve with a sense of God's mercy

We have this ministry, says the apostle, 'by the mercy of God', or 'as those who have received mercy'. In saying that he was recognising that there is nothing meritorious in the service we do for God. Our service, like our salvation, is all of his grace. To serve the Lord is our highest privilege as well as our bounden duty. Let us accept it thankfully.

We serve with clean hands

'We have renounced disgraceful, underhand ways; we refuse to practise cunning or to tamper with God's word, but by the open statement of the truth we would commend ourselves to every man's conscience in the sight of God' (verse 2). Paul is here answering the accusations of his opponents who questioned both his motives and his methods. In doing so he enunciates a principle of supreme importance in all service for Christ. Our hands must be clean; we must employ no dishonourable practices; there must be no distorting of the truth to suit our own ends. Our lives must be so transparently honest that they commend themselves to others as well as to God.

We serve as agents of Christ's gospel

All Christian service should have as its underlying motive the desire to share the good news of Christ with the world at large. Why? Because here, and indeed all through the New Testament, the world is seen as being in a state of spiritual darkness, blinded by the devil to the truth of God. And likewise the gospel is described in terms of light (verses 3–6). Paul speaks of 'the light of the good news which reveals the glory of Christ, in whom men see what God is like'. That light has shone in our hearts in order that we might reflect it—'the light which unveils the glory of God in the person of Christ'. Whatever form our service takes, we must never forget that we are light-bearers and that our object is to magnify not ourselves but the Lord as agents of his love.

We serve one another for Jesus' sake

'We proclaim Christ Jesus as Lord', says the apostle, 'and ourselves as your servants, for Jesus' sake' (verse 5). Paul felt himself to be 'the servant of the servants of God', and that too is our privilege. In exercising it we are fulfilling our Lord's new commandment of which we read in today's Gospel: 'Love one another. As I have loved you, so you are to love one another. If there is this love among you, then all will know that you are my disciples.' To love is to serve: service is love in action. And we do it 'for Jesus' sake': because he taught us, because he loved us, because we owe everything to him. Our service to one another in his name is the best way of expressing our gratitude to him and paying our debt.

ELEVENTH SUNDAY AFTER TRINITY

Christ's ambassadors

> 2 Corinthians 5.19, 20 (NEB) *'God has entrusted us with the message of reconciliation. We come therefore as Christ's ambassadors. It is as if God were appealing to you through us: in Christ's name, we implore you, be reconciled to God!'*

One of the late Dr W. Sangster's many works was entitled *Why Jesus Never Wrote a Book.* The point he made was that Jesus chose to propagate his message in the world he had redeemed not by writing it down in a book for men to read but by entrusting it to a company of dedicated disciples and charging them, '*You* will be my witnesses to the ends of the earth.' In keeping with this, in today's Gospel we hear the Lord praying for his disciples, and he says: 'Not for these alone I pray, but for those also who *through their words* put their faith in me' (St John 17.20). Clearly he envisaged his Church as a witnessing community, spreading his good news among men by word of mouth. Today's Epistle tells us something about the task and how it concerns us as servants of Christ.

We have a mission

What is that mission? What is it we are sent to do? St Paul said to the Corinthians, 'We come to you as Christ's ambassadors, as though God were appealing to you through us.' Christ's ambassadors! Here is a word-picture of those who witness for the Lord. An ambassador is the official representative of his sovereign or government at a foreign court. He is charged with authority by those who send him and has the right to speak and act on their behalf. He is therefore a man with a mission, and an important mission too. And *we* have a mission—all of us, clergy and laity alike. What is more, the mission entrusted to us involves a solemn responsibility and is invested with a heavenly dignity. Poor and unworthy though we may be in ourselves, we are envoys of the King of kings, his agents and representatives through whom he carries out his reconciling purpose in the world.

We have a motive

In fulfilling our mission as Christ's ambassadors we have a motive which urges us on. Of course, we could claim to have several motives, and earlier in this same chapter the apostle mentions one such: the thought of divine judgement to which all men are subject. 'Therefore', he says, 'knowing the fear of the Lord, we persuade men' (verse 11). But here he speaks of a stronger and more positive motive: *the love of Christ in dying to redeem us from sin* (verse 14). For as he says, 'his purpose in dying for all was that men should cease to live for themselves but for him who for their sake died and rose again'. Paul's meaning is this, that in the light of the cross we view life in a new light. We recognise how greatly we are in debt to Christ. We are no longer our own: we have been bought with a price. Therefore we bear our witness under the constraint of his love, filled not only with a sense of obligation but with a sense of gratitude.

We have a message

That message is summed up here in a single word: 'God has entrusted us with the message of reconciliation.' What a message it is! *Reconciliation* is one of the big words of the Christian gospel. No word is more apposite for our own day, living as we do in a world full of tensions where men are out of harmony with themselves, with society, and with God. Reconciliation is man's fundamental need What the apostle is stressing in this remarkable passage is that this need has been fully met in Christ and simply awaits man's acceptance. Man cannot achieve reconciliation; he can only receive it. 'From first to last this has been the work of God,' says the apostle. 'He has reconciled us men to himself through Christ, and he has enlisted us in this service of reconciliation.' And so as Christ's ambassadors we make our appeal: Be reconciled to God! This is our message. It's a timeless message, a message for today, a message for all men, and an urgent message; for 'behold, now is the day of salvation' (ch. 6.2). Let's not keep it to ourselves.

> We have a gospel to proclaim,
>   Good news for men in all the earth;
> The gospel of a Saviour's name,
>   We sing his glory, tell his worth.
>   (Edward J. Burns.)

TWELFTH SUNDAY AFTER TRINITY

Suffering as a Christian

I Peter 4.16 (NEB) *'If anyone suffers as a Christian he should feel no disgrace, but confess that name to the honour of God.'*

Anyone who reads the New Testament must see at once that there is nothing odd about a Christian suffering for his faith. Such suffering is regarded as perfectly normal. It is something to be expected. Yet we are bound to admit that for those of us living in this country at the present time suffering as a Christian is comparatively rare. Compared with the early church we have a soft and easy time of it. But Christians in other parts of the world do have to face what the apostle calls here 'the fiery ordeal' (verse 12), and perhaps our turn will come. What then? The writer has some counsel to offer us; and the first thing he says to us is this:

Don't be surprised if suffering comes

'My dear friends, do not be bewildered by the fiery ordeal that is upon you, as though it were something extraordinary.' No, there is nothing extraordinary about it. Strange as it may sound to us, suffering is 'business as usual' as far as the Church is concerned. In today's Gospel we hear Jesus warning his disciples about the kind of reception they may expect from a hostile world (John 16.1-4). The story of the Acts illustrates his words. The Church is seen to be continually up against the 'world'— whether the Jewish religious world, or the intellectual world of the Greeks, or the world of pagan superstition—and as a result it is under fire. Perhaps if we today were more like the Church of the New Testament we might have a tougher time of it. And it might do us good. It might challenge our loyalties. 'If the world has nothing to say against you,' said D. L. Moody, 'beware lest Jesus Christ has nothing to say for you.'

Regard suffering as a privilege

'If anyone suffers as a Christian, he should feel it no disgrace.' Far from that, Peter sees a certain 'glory' attached to suffering. Why? He says: 'It gives you a share of Christ's sufferings, and that is cause for joy; and when his glory is revealed, your joy will be triumphant.' This is a familiar New Testament thought. To suffer *for* Christ is to suffer *with* Christ; and to share his passion now is to partake of his triumph hereafter. Persecution is the path to glory. But there is a present glory as well for those who bear the reproach of Christ (see verse 14). To suffer for him is a privilege, not a disgrace: glory, not shame.

Be sure your suffering is undeserved

Here the apostle touches an important point. 'Be ready to suffer as a Christian—that is, because you are Christ's man—but be careful you don't suffer because of your own wrong doing. Be sure your suffering is undeserved.' So he argues. These are his actual words: 'Let none of you suffer as a murderer, or a thief, or a wrongdoer, or as a mischief-maker; yet if one suffers as a Christian, let him not be ashamed.' It is hardly likely that as Christians we shall suffer for murder or theft or any such crime. But what about mischief-making? The word (a rare one) denotes a meddlesome attitude, being a 'busybody' (AV), poking one's nose into other people's affairs. Is that unknown in Christian circles? Yet it should not happen; and if we suffer for it, we ourselves are to blame.

Trust God in your suffering

The apostle declares that suffering is a form of judgement on the Church (verse 17). By the way we react to it our faith is tested and assessed. So we must continue to trust God when suffering comes. 'Let those who suffer according to God's will do right and entrust their souls to a faithful Creator.' God is always *faithful*: he will never break his word. And he is our *Creator*: a title which reminds us that his power is able to make something even of our sufferings. There is comfort here. When we suffer we are in the hands of almighty love; and his love will never let us go.

THIRTEENTH SUNDAY AFTER TRINITY

Neighbourly love

Romans 12.9 (RSV) *'Let love be genuine.'*

So says St Paul at the beginning of today's Epistle. As a general proposition it is an excellent piece of advice. But how does this genuine love work out in practice? What is its place in ordinary everyday life? For answer we turn to the Gospel, the parable of the Good Samaritan, or as we might better call it, the parable of the Good Neighbour. For in telling it Jesus was answering the lawyer's question, 'Who is my neighbour?' In doing so he also answered a parallel question: What does it mean to love my neighbour?

Who is my neighbour?

In answer to our Lord's challenge the lawyer had quoted the words of scripture which come in our Old Testament lesson: 'You shall love your neighbour as yourself' (Leviticus 19.18). It was a correct answer and Jesus told him to go and get on with the job. But the lawyer was not content to leave it there. He said in effect, 'It's all very well to tell me to love my neighbour, but who precisely is he? How far am I expected to go? Where do I draw the line? What are the limits to neighbourliness?' It was to answer those questions that Jesus told his story. It's a story with a strangely modern ring, for it's about a man who was a victim of violence. What is more, the man was a Jew, and that too ties up with life today. But the real point is this. The man who went to his aid, after the clergy had politely passed him by, was a foreigner, a Samaritan—a man of a different race and a different religion. 'Jews have no dealing with Samaritans': that was the general rule. And equally Samaritans had no dealings with Jews. But here we see this Samaritan passer-by breaking with convention, ignoring the race regulations, and treating the wounded man simply as a fellow human being.

Plainly the world of Christ's day was very much like our own, a bitterly divided world; and in such a world the question is still relevant: 'Who is my neighbour?' It's a question that challenges Jews and Arabs in the Middle East, Coloured and White people in South Africa, Catholics and Protestants in Northern Ireland. And the answer Jesus gave 2,000 years ago remains the same. There are no limits to neighbourliness. The whole human race is one vast neighbourhood. We are to recognise as our neighbour anyone who needs our help, and whom we are able to help, irrespective of race, rank or religion. That being so, we are compelled to face our second question.

What does it mean to love my neighbour?

The answer is seen in what the Samaritan did for the man by the roadside. When he saw him he had compassion, and went to him and bound up his wounds, pouring on oil and wine; then he set him on his own beast and brought him to an inn and took care

87

of him.' Here is love in action: compassionate, costly, self-forgetting. More than that, as a good neighbour this man not only did his duty: he went the second mile; for he gave the landlord money and promised to pay any further expenses on his return. Surely this is the sort of thing St Paul meant when he said 'Let love be genuine.' The word used implies that there is a 'love' which is largely hypocritical: insincere, not real. What the apostle had in mind, as the Epistle as a whole makes clear, is love that is warm and affectionate, generous and hospitable, modest and self-effacing, considerate and forgiving.

What does it mean to love my neighbour? It means something more than just to sympathise with him, to show an interest in him, to be kindly disposed towards him. It means to get alongside him, to serve his present need, to make some sacrifice for him. And that, let us be clear, is the test of true religion. Not orthodoxy, not churchiness, not piety, but neighbourly love. But let's be sure it is the real thing. 'Let love be genuine.'

FOURTEENTH SUNDAY AFTER TRINITY

Family circle

Ephesians 5.21 (RSV) *'Be subject to one another out of reverence for Christ.'*

In no sphere of life has the Christian religion exerted a more powerful and transforming influence than in the family circle. The Christian home has been called the masterpiece of the gospel in its work of social blessing. In today's Epistle St Paul, from the starting point of mutual submission, writes about the great ideals of Christian marriage and the relationship 'in the Lord' between husbands and wives, parents and children. Fundamental to what he says is our Lord's teaching about marriage and childhood which forms the subject of the Gospel.

Christian marriage

The Christian family is the product of Christian marriage. St Paul here deals with the marriage bond in the light of the relationship of Christ to the Church. This metaphorical use of marriage is found often in the Bible to describe the union between God and his people (see the Old Testament lesson). The apostle now uses the analogy to teach wives and husbands their respective duties. On the one hand: 'Wives, be subject to your husbands, as to the Lord; for the husband is the head of the wife as Christ is the head of the church.' On the other hand: 'Husbands, love your wives, as Christ loved the church and gave himself up for her.' This conception of marriage not only lifts the subject to a high spiritual level. It also throws light on the nature of the marriage bond. For example, when Paul declares that the husband is the head of the wife he is not simply insisting upon the husband's ultimate responsibility; he is also making clear that husband and wife are complementary. The head is not complete without the body, any more than is the body without the head. So likewise husband and wife constitute a whole, a unity, a partnership, and each is necessary to the other. This partnership, as Jesus insists in the Gospel, is a permanent one, a lifelong union (St Mark 10.9).

Christian love

Christian marriage is based on Christian love. This beyond question is the outstanding point in the Epistle. True, as we have seen, the apostle tells wives to be subject to their husbands; but behind all his teaching is the idea that Christ is the heavenly bridegroom and the Church his beloved bride, so that the husband's duty as 'head' of the wife is to love her with a love like that of Christ for his own—love that is sacrificial, self-forgetting, generous, grudging nothing, giving all. And what of the wife's subjection to her husband? 'It is a subject of which love is the very soul and animating principle. In a true marriage, as in the loving obedience of a believing soul to Christ, the wife submits not because she has found a master, but because her heart has found its rest' (Maclaren).

Christian home life

Last of all Paul has something to say about family life, just as in in the Gospel Christ's teaching about the sanctity of marriage is followed by his blessing of the young children. A happy Christian marriage paves the way for a happy Christian home. Children are urged to obey their parents: not only as a matter of 'right' in accordance with the fifth commandment, but as a Christian duty 'in the Lord'. In the same spirit the apostle appeals to parents (the word 'fathers' is a comprehensive one) to bring up their children 'in the discipline and instruction of the Lord'. Paul expects the home to be a place of Christian education. Dr A. M. Hunter remarks: 'A verse like this should make every Christian parent ask himself: "Will my children later in life, wandering about in unbelief, rise up to curse me because, intent on giving them the stone of worldly success, I forgot to give them the Bread of Life?"'

FIFTEENTH SUNDAY AFTER TRINITY

The Christian and the state

Romans 13.1 (RSV) *'Let every person be subject to the governing authorities.'*

What is the Christian's relationship to the state, the governing authorities—'the powers that be', to use the AV phrase? The question is one of particular importance today and one that needs to be carefully thought out in the light of the New Testament as a whole. Today's Epistle and Gospel provide basic teaching on the subject. Both passages make clear that the duty which the Christian man owes to the state is part of the duty he owes to God; which means that normally a good Christian can be a good citizen—and no doubt should be. But the matter is not always as simple as that.

The authority of the state

Our text says, 'Let every person be subject to the governing authorities.' Why? 'For there is no authority except from God, and those that exist have been instituted by God. Therefore he who resists the authorities resists what God has appointed, and those who resist will incur judgement.' In writing like this the apostle lifts the subject from the political to the religious level. What he is asserting is that civil government is a divine ordinance. While all authority ultimately comes from God, the supreme governor, he has chosen to delegate that authority to earthly rulers who in this matter are his appointed 'ministers' or servants. Therefore they demand our obedience. To disobey them is to disobey God.

In considering Paul's teaching here certain things must be remembered. First, that he is laying down general principles, not dealing with particular cases. Second, that he is writing out of his own experience: in his work as a Christian missionary he had found the Roman government to be on the whole his friend and protector. And third, he realised the importance of Christians in his day showing themselves to be peaceful and law-abiding citizens, not anarchists (one of the charges commonly laid against them by their enemies).

The function of the state

If the state was God-given authority, that authority is given for a purpose. St Paul goes out of his way to make that plain. In urging the Christian duty of loyalty to the state he also asserts the function of the state—which is, negatively, to repress and punish evil doers, and, positively, to protect and reward those who do good (see verses 3–5). As God's servant the ruler's clear task is to uphold the law, to administer justice, to safeguard human rights and liberties, to secure for all citizens the chance to live a full and rich life .Suppose the ruler does not do this, but in fact does the very opposite: what then? The apostle does not here face that question, but the possibility is a real one, as history proves. What if there is a clash of loyalties? What if there is a choice between God and Caesar? For the Christian there can be only one answer in such a case.

The claims of the state

If the state is to fulfil its duty and render service to its citizens it must be paid. Hence the necessity of taxation, which represents the claim made by the 'authorities' on the citizens. St Paul deals with this subject in the closing verses (6, 7) and urges his readers to pay what is due; 'for', he says, 'the authorities are ministers of God, attending to this very thing'. And because they *are* God's ministers we owe them not only revenue. We owe them respect as well. What we need to remember always is that if the state has a duty to its citizens, the citizens have a duty to the state. We must accept our responsibilities as well as claim our rights. We must 'render to Caesar the things that are Caesar's, and to God the things that are God's' (Gospel); which means that as Christians we should also *pray* for those in authority, 'that we may lead a quiet and peaceable life, godly and respectful in every way' (1 Timothy 2.2).

SIXTEENTH SUNDAY AFTER TRINITY

Christianity in action

St James 1.22 *'Be doers of the word, and not hearers only, deceiving yourselves.'*

Emerson declared that a man's life is the picture-book of his creed. He meant of course that what a person does reveals more clearly than anything else what he really believes. This is the theme of the passage which forms today's Epistle. Indeed it is the theme of this entire letter of James, which has been described as a little manual of applied Christianity. Here is some good honest down-to-earth teaching which directly relates religion to life.

Hearers only

In the previous section the writer has been telling his readers to be quick to hear God's word and to receive it into their hearts. Now he adds a necessary caution: 'But be doers of the word, and not hearers only.' What he is saying in effect is something like this: 'It's good to listen to what the Bible says and to store your minds with its teaching; but that in itself is not enough. You must obey God's word; you must translate its message into practical terms; you must live out what you learn—in your home, in your work, in your community.'

James gives a telling illustration of what he means. 'A man who listens to the message but never acts upon it is like one who looks in a mirror at the face nature gave him. He glances at himself and goes away, and at once forgets what he looked like' (NEB). A swift glance in the mirror resembles the casual hearing of God's truth: it is speedily forgotten. The danger is a real one. Our Lord warns us against it in the parable of the two builders (Gospel). Both 'builders' *heard* the word of Jesus. The difference was that one acted upon them, the other did not. As church people we are constantly hearing the Bible. What difference does it make in our lives?

Lip service

James mentions another danger involving self-deception: 'A man may think he is religious, but if he has no control over his tongue, he is deceiving himself; that man's religion is futile.' He obviously has in mind the person who is outwardly religious but whose speech does not correspond to his profession. What he says is equally true of the man who makes religious talk a substitute for religious deeds. That man too deceives his heart. Bunyan represents him in *Pilgrim's Progress* in the person of Talkative. This man could discourse at length on any and every subject in the most learned and pious manner, but it was all empty sound. As Christian remarked of him, 'Religion hath no place in his heart, or house, or conduct. All he hath lieth in his tongue, and his religion is to make a noise therewith.' Jesus too had strong words to say about those whose religion is mere lip service: 'Not everyone who calls me Lord, Lord . . .' (Gospel).

93

Doers of the word

We come back then to our main theme, that religious profession and practice belong together. The one is useless without the other. So James writes: 'Religion that is pure and undefiled before God our Father is this: to care for orphans and widows in their distress, and to keep oneself unstained from the world.' He does not mean that genuine religion consists of nothing other than this. He is simply providing a couple of examples: the one social, the other personal; the one expressing itself outwardly in benevolent deeds, the other expressing itself inwardly in holiness of life. The two duties are clearly complementary. One other point may be noted. The word for 'religion' employed here (*threskeia*) has to do with religious forms and ceremonies, the outward trappings of worship. But these things are not the essence of religion. Worship is more than just churchgoing. It is life, not liturgy. It is deeds, not words.

SEVENTEENTH SUNDAY AFTER TRINITY

What shall I render?

> 2 Corinthians 8.5 (NEB) '*Their giving surpassed our expectations; for they gave their very selves, offering them in the first instance to the Lord, but also, under God, to us.*'

'What shall I render to the Lord for all his bounty to me?' asked the psalmist. Deep within the heart of all who love God is the instinct to give him something. But what? 'What can I give thee, poor as I am?' The only adequate offering is that of ourselves, and this is what God most desires, for our lives belong to him. Any other offerings we make are an outward recognition and expression of that fact. They are tokens of our trusteeship. Examples are to be found in today's scripture readings.

The firstfruit offering of the Jews

The Old Testament lesson gives instructions to the people of
Israel about the offering of the 'firstfruits'. At harvest time they
were to take the first of the fruit of the ground, put it in a basket
and present it to the priest, to be set down before the altar of the
Lord. It was intended to be a symbolic offering. The worshipper
was saying 'Thank you' to God for the gifts of harvest; but the
passage makes clear that he was also acknowledging God's
mercy in delivering the nation from Egypt and giving them a
good and fruitful land (verses 5–9). The lesson teaches us that
whatever we give to God is in virtue of the fact that we are a
redeemed people. It teaches us too that God is pleased with what
we thus offer to him. But let us not forget that *what* we give is
not so important as *how* we give. In today's Gospel Jesus has
something to say about the spirit in which we must bring our
gifts to the altar (Matthew 5.23, 24).

The lavish offering of the Macedonian Christians

Now we turn to the Epistle. Here Paul is pleading with the
Christians at Corinth for a worthy response to the relief fund he
was raising from the Gentile congregations for the impoverished
Jewish Christians in Judaea. To goad them into greater action he
tells them of the example set by the Christians in Macedonia who
from the depth of their poverty had shown themselves lavishly
open-handed. 'Going to the limit of their resources, as I can
testify, and even beyond that limit, they begged us most
insistently, and on their initiative, to be allowed to share in this
generous service to their fellow-Christians' (verses 3–4). The
Macedonians referred to were doubtless the Christians at Philippi
who were renowned for their giving (see Philippians 4.10–19).
Paul's account here of how they gave to the Jewish relief fund
is a rebuke to many of us today who are so much better off. Their
giving was joyful, spontaneous, sacrificial, and above all consecrated, for 'they gave their very selves, offering them in the
first instance to the Lord'. Does our giving to God for his work
bear any resemblance to that?

Paul has a further argument to bring to bear on the Corinthians. He has set before them the splendid example of the Macedonians. Now he points them to a higher example still. 'You know how generous our Lord Jesus Christ has been: he was rich, yet for your sake he became poor, so that through his poverty you might become rich (verse 9)'. What grace was that!

> Thou who wast rich beyond all splendour,
>   All for love's sake becamest poor;
> Thrones for a manger didst surrender,
>   Sapphire-paved courts for stable floor.

So wrote Bishop Frank Houghton. Love always gives. Giving is the test of love. The love of the Lord Jesus gave to the utmost limit, as Bethlehem and Calvary remind us. Suppose we were to view our giving in the light of what he gave to us, how would it look?

EIGHTEENTH SUNDAY AFTER TRINITY

Faith—theory and practice

Hebrews 11.1 (RSV) '*Faith is the assurance of things hoped for, the conviction of things not seen.*'

There are certain chapters of the New Testament which are distinguished by the themes with which they deal. For example, the 10th chapter of St John is known as the Good Shepherd chapter. First Corinthians chapter 15 is pre-eminently the Resurrection chapter. And beyond question this 11th chapter of Hebrews is the Faith chapter. The word faith occurs in it some 25 times. It begins by describing the nature of faith and then it illustrates how faith works by appealing to some of the great heroes of Old Testament times.

The nature of faith

'Faith is the assurance of things hoped for, the conviction of things not seen.' This has been called the only definition of faith to be found in the Bible; but in actual fact it is not so much a definition of what faith is as a description of what faith does. Faith, says the writer, does two things. First, it brings us assurance of the things to which we look forward. Second, it convinces us of the reality of things unseen. So faith is occupied with the *future*—'things hoped for'; and with the *invisible*—'things not seen'. This means that faith has to do with the eternal, spiritual world which lies beyond this world of time and space. Faith is a sort of sixth sense. Just as the eye brings us into touch with what is visible and the ear with the world of sound and the hand with things tangible, so faith brings us into contact with the spiritual realm, with things unseen and eternal. Faith gives substance to these things. It makes the unseen world real, just as real as the things that are seen. It brings the things to come within our present grasp. This, according to the writer, is the nature of faith.

The activity of faith

Theory is one thing, practice is another. How does such faith work out in practice? The writer seems to anticipate that question as he proceeds to give us a number of instances of faith in action culled from the Old Testament. He shows how the giants of Israel's history had been people whose faith took hold of God's promises concerning things to come.

There was Noah, for example: the man who 'divinely warned about the unseen future, took good heed and built an ark to save his household'. Here is an excellent illustration of the faith which has just been described. But the particular point is that Noah's faith was not simply an intellectual assent but a conviction that compelled action.

Abraham's faith was of the same character. When God's call came to him to leave the security of Ur for an unknown inheritance he readily obeyed; and 'he left home without knowing where he was going'. But mark this: if he did not know *where* he was going he did know *why* he was going. He was going because God had called him and because he believed God's promise. 'For he was looking forward to the city with firm foundations, whose architect and builder is God.'

Later came the great test of Abraham's faith as related in the Old Testament lesson. According to promise the child Isaac had been born to him and Sarah, and the promise had included the assurance that Isaac should be his heir. Yet he was bidden to offer up his son, to slay his heir—and he obeyed. 'For he reckoned that God had power even to raise from the dead—and from the dead he did, in a sense, receive him back.'

These patterns of faith are set before us to assist us in our Christian pilgrimage today. For that pilgrimage is essentially a life of faith, and faith always demands obedience. It is demonstrated in action. It is not an academic exercise but a dynamic life-changing commitment. It is easy enough to stand up in church on Sunday and say 'I believe in God'. If I really do believe, my faith will show itself in the way I live from Monday to Saturday; for faith without works is dead.

NINETEENTH SUNDAY AFTER TRINITY

Citizens of heaven

Philippians 3.19 (NEB) *'We are citizens of heaven.'*

Paul writes these words to the church at Philippi in Macedonia. Now Philippi, as Luke tells us (Acts 16.12), was a Roman colony; and a Roman colony was a sort of miniature Rome, a place which enjoyed the privileges of Roman citizenship. Therefore the words 'we are citizens of heaven' would have meant something special to the first readers of this letter. They knew the meaning of citizenship. Paul now invests the word with a higher meaning. He gives it a Christian content.

Citizens of two worlds

What does it mean to be a citizen of heaven? Let us first be clear what it does not mean. The apostle's words do not imply that because we are citizens of heaven we are not also citizens of earth. The fact is that as Christians we are citizens of two worlds, this world and the next. Therefore we must not make the mistake of detaching ourselves from the affairs of this present life, ignoring our secular rights and responsibilities, and opting out of our duty to the nation and the community. The readings for a previous Sunday (Trinity 15) have reminded us of our duty to the state. Today's Old Testament lesson teaches us the same thing. The prophet Jeremiah speaks a message to his fellow Jews who had been carried off into captivity. They were in a strange country, among an alien people; yet God's word to them was: 'Seek the welfare of the city where I have sent you into exile, and pray to the Lord on its behalf, for in its welfare you will find your welfare.' The principle is that taught by Jesus: 'Render to Caesar the things that are Caesar's, and to God the things that are God's.'

Our city-home

We fail in our duty as Christians if we do not recognise the claims of Caesar as well as of Christ. All the same, the ultimate truth is that our 'citizenship' is in heaven. The word Paul uses in this connection has the idea of a native or capital city, and he is obviously playing on this idea in writing to the Philippians who were proud of their status as a Roman colony. *Their* native city was Rome, not Philippi; and though the city was far away, they were nevertheless enrolled among its citizens. So Paul says here in effect; 'As Christians we are dwelling temporarily in this world, but our capital city is in heaven. That is where our home is, that is where we belong; and that is where our King reigns. What is more, we are looking for the return of our King, as he has promised, and when he comes he will effect our final salvation. For he will rescue us from our earthly afflictions and by his sovereign power he will transfigure our frail mortal bodies into his own glorious image, so that we may be partakers of his heavenly kingdom.'

Preparing for heaven

Such is the glittering prospect set before us. And if that hope is ours, what manner of persons ought we to be here and now? We come back to the Epistle, where Paul sees this present life as a preparation for heaven. We may think we don't know much about heaven, but this at least we know, that heaven is where God is, and God is holy. So Paul here gives his readers a call to holiness. This was all the more necessary because there were at Philippi 'enemies of the cross of Christ' who were leading sensual and gluttonous lives, with their minds set on earthly things. By contrast, as those who belong to Christ (see Gospel), we are to be different. Just because we are citizens of heaven we are to exhibit the standards of heaven in our daily conduct. We are to renounce the world and subdue the flesh. We are to keep looking to the Lord—and for the Lord—and to occupy our minds with the interests of his kingdom. This is the pattern set before us: a heavenly life in preparation for a heavenly kingdom of which we are already citizens and which is the goal of our pilgrimage.

TWENTIETH SUNDAY AFTER TRINITY

Going on with Christ

Hebrews 12.1, 2 (RSV) *'Let us run with perseverance the race that is set before us, looking to Jesus the pioneer and perfecter of our faith.'*

It is a comparatively easy thing to begin the Christian life. It is much more difficult to persevere in it from start to finish, especially when things get tough. To remain faithful to God in a largely pagan society is a costly thing, as the story of Shadrach, Meshach and Abednego teaches us (Old Testament lesson). Many begin to follow Christ but they don't go very far before giving up. Let's face this issue and ask, What are the secrets of endurance? How are we to go on with Christ? Here are three bits of counsel.

Count the cost

The first thing to do is to make up our minds that the Christian path is not a bed of roses. Before we set out on the path we ought to count the cost, for there is a price to be paid for discipleship. Henry Drummond spoke of the kingdom of God as a society and declared, 'Its entrance money is nothing; its subscription, all you have.' He meant that you enter the kingdom simply by accepting the free grace of God; you continue your membership in it by a life of total commitment—and that is likely to be a very demanding thing. Christ accepts no half-hearted followers, as today's Gospel makes plain (see St Luke 9.57–62). A man said to him in a fit of enthusiasm, 'I will follow you wherever you go'. It sounded fine; but the Lord's reply was to tell him to count the cost: 'Foxes have holes, and birds of the air have nests; but the Son of Man has nowhere to lay his head.' Another said to him, 'I will follow you, Lord; but let me first say farewell to those at my home.' This man was not prepared to give Jesus priority. His family and home circle claimed his first love. He was given a very straight answer: 'No one who puts his hand to the plough and looks back is fit for the kingdom of God.'

Have faith in God

Today's Epistle tells of the magnificent feats of endurance on the part of some of the Old Testament saints—Gideon, Samson, David and others—'who through faith conquered kingdoms, enforced justice, received promises, stopped the mouths of lions, quenched raging fire, escaped the edge of the sword, won strength out of weakness, became mighty in war, put foreign enemies to flight.' What a record of endurance! How did they do it? Not simply by their own courage and resolution but *through faith*—that is, through their trust in God. Their faith nerved them for the battle and gave them grace to hold out to the bitter end. Those who overcome the world are the men of faith: not so much because they have great faith in God, but because they have faith in a great God.

Fix your eyes on Jesus

The writer of the Epistle has pointed us to the heroes of faith in days of old. He goes on to describe them as a 'great cloud of witnesses' who surround us as we run the Christian race, like the spectators in the arena. And how are we to run? Looking to *them* and their marvellous feats of endurance? No. The writer tells us to fix our gaze elsewhere. 'Let us run with perseverance the race that is set before us, looking to Jesus the pioneer and perfecter of our faith, who for the joy that was set before him endured the cross, despising the shame, and is seated at the right hand of the throne of God' (Hebrews 12.1, 2).

The Christ of the cross is not only our Redeemer who died for our sins. He is also our leader or 'pioneer' who points the way and whom we seek to follow. When his time came he 'set his face to go to Jerusalem' (Gospel)—and he never turned back. He endured the cross. He overcame. That is why as we run the race today we must keep 'looking to Jesus' as our supreme example and our constant inspiration.

TWENTY-FIRST SUNDAY AFTER TRINITY

Holy places or holy people?

> St John 4.23 (NEB) '*The time approaches, indeed it is already here, when those who are real worshippers will worship the Father in spirit and in truth . . .. God is spirit, and those who worship him must worship in spirit and in truth.*'

Questions about worship fill the church today and tend to absorb too much of our time. Such questions are by no means new. The Samaritan woman in today's Gospel raised such a question when she said to Jesus, 'Our fathers worshipped on this mountain, but you Jews say that the temple where God should be worshipped is in Jerusalem.' In his reply Jesus directed her attention to something of more vital importance. He spoke about those who are 'real worshippers' and said that what matters is not *where* you worship but *how*—'in spirit and in truth'.

Holy places

Behind the query raised by the woman was the fact that Jews and Samaritans had different centres of worship. The Jewish temple was in Jerusalem, whereas the Samaritans had built a rival temple on Mount Gerizim. The worship in both cases was bound up with the tangible and visible: with holy places, with a priestly system of sacrifice, with outward forms and elaborate ceremonial. This kind of worship is typified on a grand and terrifying scale in the giving of the law from Mount Sinai— today's Old Testament lesson which is also referred to in the Epistle (Exodus 19.16–24; Hebrews 12.18–21). The mountain shook, wrapped in fire and smoke and darkness, and there were lightnings, thunderings and trumpet blasts as God revealed himself in majesty and spoke his commandments. The people, filled with terror, were compelled to keep their distance. One thing clearly the scene typified, and that is what Dr Barclay has called 'the absolute unapproachability of God'. God was hidden in darkness. The way to him was barred. Man must keep his distance. To attempt to draw near meant death. Such, in vivid pictorial form, was the worship of the old covenant.

Holy people

We come back to the story of Jesus and the woman at the well. She had talked about worship. It is significant that he spoke to her about *worshippers*. She was interested in places; his concern was with *people*. He made it clear that the key to worship is not where you worship but how: that 'God is spirit, and those who worship him must worship in spirit and in truth'. These are the 'real worshippers'. Holy people matter more than holy places. Cowper wrote:

> Jesus, where'er thy people meet,
> There they behold thy mercy-seat;
> Where'er they seek thee thou art found,
> And every place is hallowed ground.

Of course, just because we are body as well as spirit, we may use outward and visible things as aids to worship, and essentially so in the gospel sacraments; but we must not forget that sanctity attaches not to places but to people, and that the most magnificent 'worship' may be nothing but a piece of empty pageantry unless it is offered 'in spirit and in truth'.

What does that mean? To worship *in spirit* is to worship in the depths of our being—inwardly and not merely outwardly. True worship is man's regenerate spirit holding communion with the Spirit of the living God. The latter part of the Epistle provides a glimpse of such worship: worship which is concerned with the spiritual world, the 'heavenly Jerusalem', and which enables the worshippers to keep company with the angelic hosts and 'the first-born citizens of heaven'—that is, the heirs of salvation—as they draw near to 'God the judge of all' with perfect confidence through 'Jesus the mediator of the new covenant' and the merits of his atoning sacrifice (verses 22–24).

And to worship *in truth*? That is to worship in accordance with divine revelation, in harmony with that unveiling of truth which God has given us in Christ, and not to follow our own speculations and ideas.

TWENTY-SECOND SUNDAY
AFTER TRINITY

Life in the local church

> I Thessalonians 5.12 (NEB) '*We beg you, brothers, to acknowledge those who are working so hard among you, and in the Lord's fellowship are your leaders and counsellors.*'

In today's Epistle St Paul paints a picture in miniature. It is a picture of life in the local church—in this case the church at Thessalonica in Greece. It was a newly formed congregation and the members were all recent converts. All the same the picture given here probably reflects the local church scene as it was in the apostle's day. Incomplete as the picture must be, it offers us a glimpse of three aspects of church life in those far-off days: its leadership, fellowship, and worship. These matter have meaning for us in our own church life.

The church's leadership

The passage begins, in the words of our text, with a call to church members to respect their pastors—'those who are over you in the Lord', as RSV—and to 'hold them in the highest possible esteem and affection for the work they do'. It is interesting to note that the Thessalonian church, though so recently established, was already sufficiently organised to have its own 'clergy' as we should call them. But the distinction between clergy and laity was not so sharp then as it is now; and in any case these 'elders' or presbyters were very different from most modern parsons. They were local men, chosen from the congregation and set apart for a ministry of pastoral oversight. They received no stipend but earned their living in secular employment and exercised their ministry in their spare time. But they took their ministry seriously and were doing a good job. Paul commends them for their hard work. Clearly the church at Thessalonica owed much to their devotion and diligence. Happy the church that is blessed with faithful leadership and where there is a relationship of mutual respect and affection between pastors and people.

The church's fellowship

Paul's next exhortation is, 'Be at peace among yourselves'. That may sometimes be harder than it sounds. The Christians who make up a congregation are necessarily a mixed body and it is not always easy to maintain the fellowship of the Spirit in the bond of peace. But it's important all the same, for a divided church cannot give a good witness in a divided world.

If the fellowship is to be strong and healthy some members of the church need particular help; so Paul goes on: 'We urge you, brothers, to admonish the careless, encourage the faint-hearted, support the weak, and be very patient with them all'. And what's to be done when there are differences and disputes, when one member has a grievance against another? 'See to it that no one pays back wrong for wrong, but always aim at doing the best you can for each other and for all men.' The church must be a fellowship of reconciliation. Wrongs must be forgiven. Love must prevail.

The church's worship

The passage ends with a call to worship. 'Be always joyful; pray continually; give thanks whatever happens.' Here are some of the elements which find expression in public worship: joy in singing God's praise, prayer for others as well as for ourselves, and thanksgiving for mercies received—including the church's greatest thanksgiving, the holy eucharist. The apostle continues: 'Do not stifle inspiration, and do not despise prophetic utterances'. This seems to be a reference to preaching, and inspired preaching at that. So here is another element in worship—the sermon. And last of all comes the benediction: 'May the God of peace sanctify you wholly; and may your spirit and soul and body be kept sound and blameless at the coming of our Lord Jesus Christ.' We add our own *amen* to that and say, 'He who calls us is faithful, and he will do it'.

TWENTY-THIRD SUNDAY AFTER TRINITY

Fifth before Advent

Maker of heaven and earth

Genesis 1.1 (RSV) '*In the beginning God created the heavens and the earth.*'

That is how the Bible begins. The Apostles' Creed, being very much a 'Bible in brief', begins in the same way, with the doctrine of creation. 'I believe in God the Father Almighty, Maker of heaven and earth.' Here is a theme worthy of our consideration today, difficult though we may find it. Indeed it is beyond our finite minds and can only be understood from the standpoint of faith: 'By faith we understand that the world was created by the word of God, so that what is seen was made out of things which do not appear' (Hebrews 11.3). As we reflect on the subject in the light of the biblical teaching let us see what it says to us about God, Christ, and the Church.

God the Creator

'In the beginning God created the heavens and the earth.' We must be clear at the outset that the Genesis record is not a scientific but a religious account of creation, set out in pictorial form. It does not tell us everything, but it does stress certain basic facts. For example, it establishes that the universe had a beginning in time and that matter is not eternal; that the world did not come into being by chance but by the will and power of God; that creation is not to be thought of as a single act but as a long process and a progressive development; that God is transcendent, self-existent and self-sufficient, distinct from his creation and independent of it; that man is the crown of creation, made in the image of God and for his glory; and that the world is God's world, and that everything he made is good.

A right view of creation gives us a new conception of the wisdom, majesty and love of God. It also enables us to appreciate the glories of nature as his handiwork; and it teaches us to care for the world and every living thing in it.

Christ the agent of creation

So far we have stopped short at the Old Testament. Now we must go farther and ask, Where does Christ come into all this? Today's Epistle supplies the answer. In one of the most profound passages in the New Testament St Paul speaks of Christ in relation to God and the created order. 'He is the image of the invisible God; his is the primacy over all created things. In him everything in heaven and earth was created . . .: the whole universe has been created through him and for him. And he exists before everything, and all things are held together in him' (Colossians 1.15–17). What the apostle is saying is this:

that when in the beginning God created the heavens and the earth, Christ was there and Christ was at work. He is the divine agent through whom the whole creative process was carried out. More than that, he is not only God's mediator in creation. He is also creation's goal: the whole universe was created *for* him. And again, he is the sustainer of it all, for in him the entire created order holds together.

Here is a magnificent view of our Lord. He is the cosmic Christ, the Lord of creation, prior in time and dignity to all things, 'the principle of cohesion in the universe,' as Bishop Lightfoot put it, the One who 'impresses upon creation that unity and solidarity which makes it a cosmos instead of a chaos'.

The Church, the new creation

The apostle leads us on further still, from the old creation to the new, from the natural order to the spiritual. Christ is not only Lord of the universe. He is also Lord of the Church by virtue of his incarnation, death and resurrection. 'In him the complete being of God came to dwell', Paul asserts, and 'through him God chose to reconcile the whole universe to himself, making peace through the shedding of his blood upon the cross' (verses 19, 20). And as a result of that sacrificial work the Church, the new creation, the Body of Christ, was born: that order of society which acknowledges Christ as supreme Head, and through which he manifests himself to men and does his work in the world. Of all God's creative achievements, the Church is the most wonderful of all—and the most costly.

TWENTY-FOURTH SUNDAY
AFTER TRINITY

Fourth before Advent

What is man?

Genesis 3.15 (RSV) '*I will put enmity between you and
the woman, and between your seed and her seed; he shall
bruise your head, and you shall bruise his heel.*'

What is man? The question is asked twice in the psalms, and
in each case it receives a different answer. In Psalm 8 the answer
is given in terms of man's dignity and worth, as one made only
a little less than God himself, crowned with glory and honour.
Psalm 144 takes the opposite viewpoint. Here man is seen in his
littleness and insignificance, a mere creature of time: 'man is
like a breath, his days are like a passing shadow'. We need to
keep both answers in mind if we are to form a right assessment
of man; for the Bible is concerned with man both as God made
him and intended him to be, and as man has made himself
through his own wrong-doing.

The fact of sin

In any realistic understanding of human nature we cannot
escape the hard fact that man is a sinner with a nature that is
morally perverted. You haven't got to read the Bible to discover
that unpalatable truth. You have only to read the newspaper—or
for that matter, your own heart. All too plainly there is something tragically wrong with man at the very depths of his being.
He has 'fallen' from the state in which God made him. God made
him, with all creation, 'very good'. But he is no longer in that
happy condition. He is often very bad. Sin, an alien element, has
entered into his life and has estranged him from his Creator—as
the pictorial record of Genesis 3 makes plain. There we see man,
who was made for fellowship with God, discrediting God's
word, doubting his love, hiding from his presence—and at last
driven out of Paradise. This is the Bible portrait of man in his

fallen and rebellious state. It is not past history but present experience. Jesus said much the same in his parable of the Prodigal Son. 'Man is not at home in his Father's house, but a needy outcast in a far country' (J. S. Whale).

The nature of sin

The Genesis story does not tell us of the origin of evil itself, but it does throw light on the nature of sin. Among other things it teaches us that sin is not part of man's natural condition but is an intruder; that it is not God's work but the devil's; that it arises out of the misuse of man's freedom; and that its essential characteristic is man's repudiation of God's word and authority and the assertion of his own self-will and independence. Hence in the New Testament sin is defined quite simply as 'lawlessness' (1 St John 3.4): man's violation of God's law. St Paul in today's Epistle enlarges on the relation between sin and the law and shows how the law, good and holy as it is, makes man conscious of sin, and even provokes him to sin (Romans 7.7–12). What the apostle writes contains various echoes of the story of the Fall.

The conquest of sin

The picture so far has been a sombre one. It could not be otherwise, for we have been dealing with sin, and sin is Public Enemy Number One. But sin is not all-powerful and man's condition is not hopeless. Sin has not the final word. Sin has met its master. God's promise to fallen man was that a deliverer would come. To the tempter he said: 'I will put enmity between you and the woman, and between your seed and her seed; he shall bruise your head, and you shall bruise his heel.' The rest of the Bible is virtually the unfolding and fulfilment in history of that promise, until at length, 'when the fullness of time came, God sent forth his Son, born of a woman, born under the law, to redeem those under the law'. Christ is the woman's Seed, God's incarnate Son, man's Saviour. This is the good news. 'For God so loved the world, that he gave his only Son . . .'

O loving wisdom of our God!
When all was sin and shame,
A second Adam to the fight
And to the rescue came.

TWENTY-FIFTH SUNDAY
AFTER TRINITY

Third before Advent

God's elect

Genesis 12.1–3 (RSV, mg.) '*The Lord said to Abram,
"Go away from your country and your father's house to
the land that I will show you. And I will make of you
a great nation, and I will bless you . . . and in you all the
families of the earth will be blessed.*'

When did the Church begin? In answer, most people would
probably say that the Church was born on the day of Pentecost
with the coming of the Holy Spirit. But at best that is only a
half-truth. The Bible doctrine of the Church has its roots
firmly embedded in the Old Testament and goes back to the
time of Abraham, who was chosen to be the father of the Jewish
nation. Here in today's Old Testament lesson we see God working out his purpose for his people, and through his people for
the world.

The call of Abraham

Abraham came originally from Ur of the Chaldees, and it was
while he was there that the call of God had come to him: 'Go
from your country and your kindred and your father's house
to the land that I will show you.' With that call the history of
redemption begins. God speaks: man responds. Yet it could not
have been easy for Abraham to respond: to forsake the known
for the unknown, to exchange the comfort of life in a civilised

society for a nomad's existence in a foreign land. Nevertheless he obeyed the call. He took God at his word and ventured forth: 'by faith he went out, not knowing where he was to go' (Hebrews 11.8). This is of the very essence of faith, for ourselves as well as for Abraham. For faith, as A. M. Hunter comments, 'is a taking of God at his word—an Abraham-like obedience, in face of all odds, to the God who reveals himself to us. Now, since God has revealed himself to us decisively in Christ, Christian faith is a taking of God at his word in Christ: to live no more by reliance on our own resources, but only by trust in his saving grace offered to us in Christ.'

The People of God

Attached to God's call to Abraham to leave his country was a series of promises, beginning with: 'I will make of you a great nation, and I will bless you, and make your name great, so that you will be a blessing.' In saying that God was in effect declaring his purpose to create a people for his own possession—his Israel. The 'great nation' to be formed out of Abraham's offspring was in fact the church of the Old Testament: the people God chose for himself, to whom he revealed himself and gave his law, and with whom he entered into covenant. And that church persisted, amid much failure and apostasy, through the centuries of history, until the coming of Jesus the Messiah. It was he who created from the Jewish church, the offspring of Abraham, the new People of God, the true Israel; and on the day of Pentecost, as he had promised, the Church was reborn by the baptism of the Spirit, to become a universal fellowship of faith and love.

The blessing of the nations

It is always important to recognise the continuity of the New Testament Church with that of the Old and to remember (as Paul emphasises in today's Epistle) that Abraham is the spiritual father of *all* the faithful, gentiles as well as Jews. In this sense Abraham rejoiced to see the day of Christ (Gospel). God's promise to him was, 'in you all the families of the earth will be blessed'. That promise never came true in Old Testament times.

The ancient people of Israel enjoyed God's blessing but failed to share it with others. Then Christ came and abolished the distinction between Israel and the rest of mankind. His gospel was for the whole world. He opened the kingdom of heaven to all believers. As St Paul argues, the promised 'blessing' depends on *faith*, not on the law, and it avails for everyone who trusts in Christ the risen Lord. For us this is a mere commonplace. In the apostle's day it was a revolutionary truth. But let us beware of complacency, lest like the old Israel we are content to keep the blessing to ourselves and fail to pass on the good news of God's love to all the world.

TWENTY-SIXTH SUNDAY AFTER TRINITY

Second before Advent

Redemption

> Exodus 3.7, 8 (RSV) *'The Lord said, "I have seen the affliction of my people who are in Egypt, and have heard their cry because of their taskmasters; I know their sufferings, and I have come down to deliver them."'*

Last Sunday's Old Testament lesson focused our attention on the call of Abraham, who typifies the man of faith. Today's is about the call of Moses, who stands out as the type of a redeemer or deliverer. It was he whom God chose to rescue his people Israel from their Egyptian captivity and bring them into the land of Caanan. Here is the beginning of the story, which finds its culmination in the passover event and points onward to a greater redemption and a greater than Moses.

Israel in Egypt

The background of the story is Israel in Egypt. The people were in bondage and misery, Pharaoh's slaves. Their lot was hard in the extreme and humanly speaking they were hopeless as well as helpless. Then, just as things were at their worst, God intervened in the situation. He appeared to Moses at the burning bush—emblem of God's blazing holiness and inextinguishable love—and spoke to him in tones of great tenderness of Israel's tragic plight. 'I have seen the affliction of my people in Egypt', he said, 'and have heard their cry because of their taskmaster, and I know all about their sufferings.'

Here is a revelation of grace. *My people* God calls them—not merely the people of Israel; and in simple homely language we are told that his eye saw their cruel oppression, his ear heard their anguished cry, and his heart felt for their grievous sufferings. God is not indifferent to human need. It is always a comfort to remember that when we are in trouble. He knows. He loves. He cares. We are his people; and best of all, he is our God.

The promise of redemption

God did more than care for his people. He said to Moses, 'I have come down to deliver them out of the hand of the Egyptians, and to bring them up out of that land to a good and broad land'—that is, Canaan. The language suggests that hitherto God had seen his people's misery from afar but that now he had 'come down' into the midst of their situation to rescue them from their foes. But how was it to be done? God had his man prepared for the job. 'Come,' he said to Moses, 'I will send you to Pharaoh, that you may bring forth my people out of Egypt.' It's hardly surprising that Moses shrank from so gigantic a task and protested loudly. But God answered his fears with the assurance of his presence, 'I will be with you', and by giving him a fresh unveiling of the divine character as disclosed in the ineffable name *Yahweh*—'I AM WHO I AM.' That name speaks of God in the mystery of his being as the living God, eternal, unchanging, immutable, mighty to save.

A greater than Moses

We are not at this point concerned with the subsequent story of the passover and the exodus. But we ought to note that that divine act of rescue and liberation is seen in the Bible as the decisive turning-point in Israel's history and as a picture in miniature of the greater redemption God accomplished for mankind through his Son, who is 'deemed worthy of greater honour than Moses' (see today's Epistle). 'Christ our passover lamb has been sacrificed for us.' 'The blood that ransomed us was that of a Lamb without spot or blemish.' 'We have our redemption through his blood.' In terms like these the New Testament speaks of Christ's saving work and in doing so it takes us back to Moses and the passover. The blood-red line of redemption runs all through the Bible from start to finish and is the theme of the Church's worship in heaven as on earth. 'Worthy is the Lamb who was slain, to receive power and wealth and wisdom and might and honour and glory and blessing!'

SUNDAY NEXT BEFORE ADVENT

The few

> 1 Kings 19.18 (RSV) *'I will leave seven thousand in Israel, all the knees that have not bowed to Baal, and every mouth that has not kissed him.'*

One of the significant truths that shines out from the pages of scripture is that God works through minorities. His actions are not tied by majority votes or mass movements. Human history illustrates the same truth. We recall Churchill's famous words of those who saved their nation in the Battle of Britain: 'Never in the field of human conflict have so many owed so much to so few.' God also has his few, the faithful minority, Christ's 'little flock', through whom he maintains his cause in the world. Today's readings all have something to say on the subject. Three injunctions sum up their message.

Be faithful

First of all, remember the story of Elijah in the idolatrous days of king Ahab. In the memorable scene on Mount Carmel Elijah had defied the prophets of Baal and vindicated the name of the Lord. But afterwards, pursued by the threats of the wicked queen Jezebel, he had lost heart and run away. When rebuked by the Lord for what he had done he bitterly complained of Israel's complete apostasy. 'They have broken thy covenant, thrown down thy altars, and slain thy prophets with the sword; and I, even I only, am left.' Poor Elijah! No wonder he was thoroughly discouraged! He thought that he alone of all his nation had remained true to God. But God's answer was this: 'I will leave seven thousand in Israel, all the knees that have not bowed to Baal, and every mouth that has not kissed him.'

Here is born the idea of the remnant. Doubtless the 7,000 was a symbolical number, small in comparison with the entire nation but nevertheless significant. Even in Ahab's day the Lord had his faithful people. So it has continued through history. God has never left himself without witness. His cause has survived the darkest hours through the loyalty of the few. That is true of the Church today as well as in the past. The message to us when we are tempted to despair is, Be faithful and never lose heart.

Be humble

We turn next to the Epistle. Here St Paul is addressing the church at Rome which was largely a Gentile congregation with only a sprinkling of Jewish believers. It seems that the Gentiles were inclined to look askance at the Jews because as a whole they had proved faithless to God and had rejected their Messiah, while *they*, the Gentiles, had taken Israel's place as the People of God. The apostle finds it necessary to warn them against spiritual pride. Salvation, he reminds them, is a matter of grace, not of race. He tells them that the Jews had lost their status through lack of faith—'and by faith *you* hold your place. Put away your pride, and be on your guard!' (Romands 11.20, 21).

The warning is also for us. Don't let us pride ourselves on our faithfulness when many are failing. It is true, we are God's people. But we are such only by his grace; and by faith we too stand. The apostle would say to us, as he did to the Roman Christians, 'Put away your boasting. There is no place for pride.

Remember God's goodness, be grateful for all that he has done for you, and be humble.'

Be vigilant

In the Gospel Jesus calls us to vigilance. He bids us remember what happened in the days of Noah when God's judgement took the godless world by surprise. The mass of people, in the midst of their busy, materialistic lives, were swept away by the flood and perished. Only a remnant was saved. And Jesus says, 'That is how it will be when the Son of Man comes.' So what? His message is plain. 'Keep awake,' he says, 'for you do not know on what day your Lord is to come' (St Matthew 24.42).

It's easy enough to grow slack in the Christian life: to drift along with the crowd, to lose our sense of mission, to forget that our redemption is drawing near. So as another Church's year comes to an end and we prepare for Advent, the call comes to us to be alert and awake, to watch and pray. The Lord is at hand.